Us

# Card Games to Play

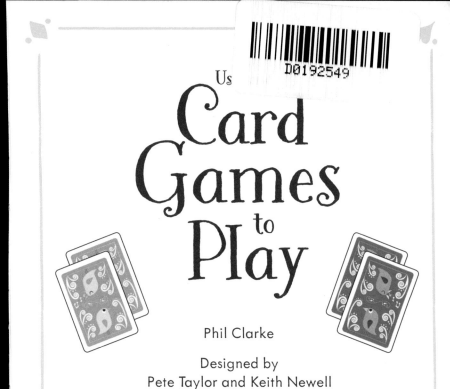

Phil Clarke

Designed by
Pete Taylor and Keith Newell

Illustrated by Jim Field

Edited by Sam Taplin

# A deck of cards

**Hearts**

**Clubs**

**Diamonds**

**Spades**

**Jokers**

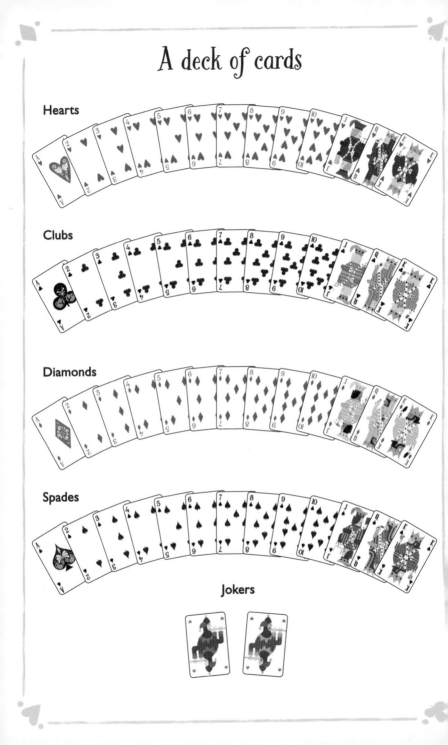

# Contents

4 Introduction

5 Blink

6 Snap

7 Advanced snap

8 Old maid

9 Pairs

10 Go fish

12 Go boom

14 Pig

15 Spoons

16 Animal snap

18 Cheat

19 Chase the Ace

20 Slapjack

21 Sevens

22 James Bond

24 Rolling stone

26 Linger longer

28 Stealing bundles

30 President

32 Muggins

34 Snip Snap Snorum

36 Ten-Ten-Five-One

38 Golf

40 Thirteens

41 Bristol solitaire

42 Martha patience

43 Catch the Ten

44 Chinese Ten

46 Simple rummy

48 Classic rummy

49 Cucumber

50 Jubilee

52 Thirty-one

54 Crazy Eights

56 Kings' corners

58 Egyptian rat slap

60 Racing demon

62 Knockout whist

64 Oh well!

66 Garbage

68 Stops

70 Pip-pip!

72 Commerce

74 Gin rummy

76 Shed

78 Bonkers

82 Durak

84 GOPS

85 Yaniv

88 Twenty-one

91 Hearts

92 Spades

94 Texas hold'em poker

101 Canasta

108 Words used in card games

112 Index of games

# Introduction

Welcome to the world of card games. This book contains more than fifty fun games with step-by-step instructions for each one. Some games need a few extras, such as a pen and paper, or counters, but most of them can be played with just a deck or two of cards.

The games are arranged in order of difficulty from the very simplest, such as snap and go fish, to more challenging ones like poker and canasta.

The instructions may use some words you don't know. Here are two important ones:

**Rank** is the order of the cards. A Jack ranks above a 10, a Queen above a Jack, and a King above a Queen.

**Value** is what a card is worth in a particular game, usually for scoring points or penalties.

If you find another word you don't know, there's a list of words used in card games on page 108. If you're looking for a particular game, the index on the last page lists them all in alphabetical order.

Have fun!

# Blink

| Players | 2 |
|---------|---|
| Difficulty | Very easy |
| Deck | 52 cards |
| Goal | To get rid of all your cards |

This simple game should be played as fast as you can – blink and you'll miss your chance.

**1.** Shuffle the cards and deal them equally between both players. Each player fans out their cards in their hands so they can see them but the other player can't.

**2.** The first player puts down any card they choose face up in the middle.

**3.** Either player can put down the next card. It must either match the rank of the first card, or be from the same suit, for example, a 10 for a 10, or a Spade for a Spade.

*The 10♠ can be followed by any 10 or any Spade.*

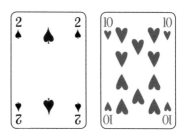

**4.** The game continues with both players racing to put their cards down on the pile as quickly as possible.

**5.** The winner is the first person to put down all their cards.

# Snap

| Players | 2–6 |
| --- | --- |
| Difficulty | Very easy |
| Deck | 52 cards |
| Goal | To win all the cards by matching ranks |

This famous game is a competition to see who has the fastest reactions.

**1.** Shuffle the cards and deal them all to the players.

**2.** Put your cards face down in a pile in front of you.

**3.** One at a time, the players take turns to turn over the top card of their pile and put it face up on a pile in the middle. Hold your cards at the top corner and turn them **away** from you: no sneaky peeking before everyone else has a chance!

**4.** If a card matches the rank of the card below, the first person to call out "Snap!" wins the whole pile in the middle, and adds it to the bottom of their face-down pile.

*Match the rank and call out "Snap!" to win the pile.*

**5.** The winner plays a card to start a new pile, and the game continues.

**6.** Anyone who runs out of cards is out.

**7.** The last player left in is the winner.

# Advanced snap

In this more challenging version, you wait until the third card is turned over, then instead of trying to match it to the last card played, you have to **match it to the one before** that. If you say "Snap!" wrong, you have to give two cards to each of the other players, which they add to the bottom of their piles.

# Old maid

| | |
|---|---|
| **Players** | 2+ |
| **Difficulty** | Very easy |
| **Deck** | 51 cards (remove a Queen); 6+ players: 2 decks |
| **Goal** | To get rid of all your cards, and not to be left with the last Queen (the 'old maid') |

In old maid you get rid of your cards by making pairs.

**1.** Shuffle the cards well, and deal them all out.

**2.** Sort your hand by rank, then discard all pairs of equal rank face down into a joint discard pile. If you are left with no cards, you are 'safe' and take no further part in this game.

*To prepare your hand, remove all matching pairs. If you have three of a kind, one remains in your hand.*

**3.** The dealer plays first, spreading out her hand and offering it face down to the player on her left. That player picks a card without looking at it, and adds it to his hand.

**4.** If the second player can now make a pair with another card in his hand, he discards the pair. Then he offers his cards to the player on his left, and so on.

**5.** The game ends when everyone is safe except for the player holding the old maid (the last Queen), who loses.

# Pairs

| | |
|---|---|
| **Players** | 2+ |
| **Difficulty** | Very easy |
| **Deck** | 52 cards |
| **Goal** | To match the most pairs |

Playing pairs is great for improving your memory.

**1.** Shuffle the cards and deal them face down on the table (or floor) in a random fashion.

**2.** The first player turns over any two cards and shows them to everyone else.

**3.** If these cards have the same rank, for example, two Jacks, the player puts them face down in front of him, then turns over two more cards. If they don't match, he turns them face down again in exactly the same place, and his turn ends.

**4.** The game continues with players taking turns to find as many matching pairs as they can, until all of the cards have been picked up. Whoever has the most pairs wins.

# Go fish

| Players | 2–6 |
| --- | --- |
| Difficulty | Very easy |
| Deck | 52 cards |
| Goal | To collect the most 'books' of four cards |

In this game you collect sets of cards, known as 'books', by asking the other players for them.

**1.** Shuffle the cards, then deal five to each player, or seven if there are only two players, then put the rest face down in the middle to make a stock pile.

**2.** Everyone looks at their cards, keeping them secret.

At the start of a game

Sophia

Jayden

Stock pile

Joss

Laila

**3.** The player left of the dealer asks another player if they have any cards of the same rank as one of their own cards. They can't ask for cards if they don't have a matching one.

**4.** If the player does have any cards of that rank, then they must hand them all over. For example, Joss asks Sophia if she has any Kings. She has the King ♣ so she hands it over.

**5.** The first player then gets to continue, by asking any of the other players for a card.

**6.** If a player doesn't have a card of the rank asked for, they say "Go fish" and the first player has to pick up a card from the middle. It's now the next player's turn.

**7.** Once you have a set of four cards of the same rank (a **book**), put it face down in front of you. For example, Laila has two 7s. She asks Joss if he has any. He gives her his 7♠. Laila then asks Sophia if she has any. She says "Go fish," so Laila takes a card from the middle. She's in luck: it's the fourth 7, so she puts down her book and goes again.

Completed book

**8.** If you have no cards left, you take one from the middle to stay in the game.

**9.** When the cards in the middle run out, the game ends. The player with the most books wins.

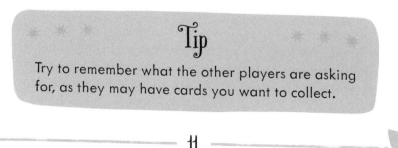

## Tip

Try to remember what the other players are asking for, as they may have cards you want to collect.

# Go boom

| | |
|---|---|
| **Players** | 2+ |
| **Difficulty** | Very easy |
| **Deck** | 52 cards (for 7+ players, combine two decks) |
| **Goal** | To get rid of all your cards |
| **Ranks** | Aces are high |

Go boom is a simple game where you get rid of cards by matching rank or suit.

**1.** Shuffle, then deal seven cards each. The rest go down in the middle. Take turns to deal.

**2.** Arrange your hands by rank, from Ace high to 2 low.

**3.** The player to the dealer's left plays any card he likes.

**4.** Each player then tries to match the rank or suit of the last card. For example, the Ace♠ could be followed by either another Ace, or another Spade.

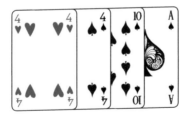

*You have to match the last card played, by rank or by suit.*

**5.** If you can't match, you have to draw a card from the middle until you can. If the cards have run out, just say "Pass" and end your turn. (For 4+ players using only one deck: pass if you draw three cards without a match.)

**6.** When everyone has played, whoever played the highest card wins, and leads (plays first) in the next round. In a draw, whoever played the highest card first wins. In the example on page 12, the player who led with the Ace♠ is the winner, so they lead again.

**7.** The dealer clears away the cards played that round into a face-down discard pile, and the winner continues the game. The moment somebody plays their last card, they call out "Boom!" and win the game.

**Example: at the end of a game**

Discard pile

Caleb

Ruby

Zach

Sarah

Zach plays his last card, the 5♦, and goes "Boom!"

**8.** If you want to play more games, you can keep score by awarding the winners points for the cards left in the other players' hands: 10 for picture cards; 1 for Aces; face value for number cards. The first to 200 points is the winner.

# Pig

| | |
|---|---|
| **Players** | 3+ |
| **Difficulty** | Very easy |
| **Deck** | Find four cards of the same rank for each player |
| **Goal** | To collect four of a kind, or spot others doing so |

This is a simple game of matching and passing cards.

**1.** To prepare the deck, you need four matching cards for each player. For example, with four players, you could use all the Aces, Kings, Queens and Jacks, leaving out the rest.

**2.** Choose a dealer. Shuffle, and deal four cards each.

**3.** All at the same time, you pick a card to discard and place it face down on your left.

**4.** You then pick up the card the player on your right discarded. You can't have more than four cards in your hand at any time.

Example of play

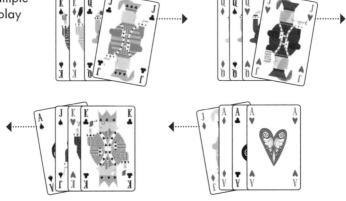

**5.** You continue like this until one player has four matching cards. At that point, she places her cards face down in front of her and silently puts her finger on her nose. As soon as the others see her do it, they put their finger on their nose, too. The last to touch their nose is the 'pig' and is out.

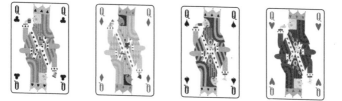

*You need to collect four of a kind.*

**6.** When someone becomes a pig and goes out, the new dealer discards one set of four cards before he reshuffles the deck and deals to the remaining players. The last two players in are joint winners.

**7.** If there are only a few players, make the game last longer by giving each player three lives, one for each letter of the word 'PIG'. So, the first time you lose you're on 'P', then 'PI', and you're out when 'PIG' is spelled in full.

## Spoons

To play a version of this game called Spoons, you need a spoon for every player but one. The spoons go in the middle, and the players grab them instead of putting their fingers on their noses. The one left with no spoon is out, or loses a life. When someone goes out, remove one spoon from the pile and one set of four cards.

# Animal snap

| Players | 4–8 |
|---|---|
| Difficulty | Very easy |
| Deck | 52 cards |
| Goal | To win all the cards |

This noisy game takes snap to a new level of silliness.

**1.** Each player chooses their own animal noise to make. Go around the circle a few times, all making your noises, so that everyone is sure which player is which animal.

**2.** Shuffle, then deal all the cards. You don't look at them, but put them in a pile face down in front of you.

**3.** The player on the dealer's left turns over a card to start a face-up pile left of his face-down pile. You all take turns to do the same, moving left. Watch closely to see if a card being turned up matches any card on top of a face-up pile. If it does, call out the noise of **the player with the matching card** twice: "Woof! Woof!" Then take their face-up pile and put it under your face-down pile.

Face-up pile

Face-down pile

**4.** If other players spot the match at the same time, then whoever finishes making the noise first wins the pile.

**5.** If someone makes the wrong noise, or makes it when it's not a match, they have to hand over one card to each player from their face-up pile.

Sheep

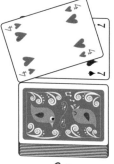

Cow

Moo! Moo! Wait,
I mean Baaa...

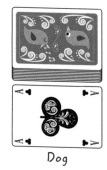

Dog

Cat

**6.** If your face-down pile runs out, just turn over your face-up pile and start again. If you run out of cards, you're out.

**7.** Players keep on turning over cards and looking for matches until just one has all the cards, and wins.

# Cheat

| | |
|---|---|
| **Players** | 3–14 |
| **Difficulty** | Very easy |
| **Deck** | 52 cards; 8+ players: two decks |
| **Goal** | To get rid of all your cards |

In this game you are allowed to cheat – as long as you don't get caught!

**1.** Deal all the cards. It doesn't matter if everyone has exactly the same number. Sort your cards by rank.

**2.** The player left of the dealer places 1–4 cards of the same rank **face down** in the middle, and announces what they are – for example, "Three 10s." But you can also cheat and play any cards you like, pretending they're all the same.

**3.** If you think someone is cheating, you say "Cheat!" and they have to show the cards. If they were cheating, they pick up all the cards in the middle and add them to their hand. If they weren't cheating, you have to pick up the whole pile. If there is more than one accuser, the first one to shout counts.

*Three tens*

*Cheat!*

**4.** If nobody thinks there was cheating, you say nothing and continue taking turns, either telling the truth or cheating.

**5.** The first out of cards wins.

# Chase the Ace

| Players | 4–8 |
| --- | --- |
| Difficulty | Very easy |
| Deck | 52 cards |
| Extras | Three counters per player (see page 110 for ideas) |
| Goal | To avoid having the lowest card |
| Ranks | Aces are low |

In this game, you need three counters for your three lives.

**1.** Shuffle, and deal one card each. The player left of the dealer decides if her card is high enough not to lose. If she wants to keep it, she says "**Stand**" and the next player goes.

**2.** If it's a low card, such as as an Ace, she says "**Change**" and tries to swap it with the player on her left. That player must swap unless he has a King, which he turns face up.

**3.** On his turn, the dealer can stand, or change by placing his card under the stock and taking the top card. If the top card is a King, he cannot take it.

**4.** You all show your cards. Whoever has the lowest card loses a life. If it's a tie, more than one player loses a life. The player left of the dealer deals the next round.

**5.** When a player loses all her lives, she is out. The last player in is the winner. If all the remaining players tie for lowest card, they keep their lives and play again.

# Slapjack

| Players | 4–10 |
| --- | --- |
| Difficulty | Very easy |
| Deck | 52 cards |
| Goal | To win all the cards |
| Values | Aces are low |

This fast, funny game involves a lot of slapping.

**1.** Shuffle, and deal all the cards. Don't look at your cards but keep them in a pile face down in front of you.

**2.** Taking turns from the dealer's left, you play the top card of your pile face up into the middle. As in **snap** (page 6), you flip the card away from you, so you don't see it before anyone else. This should be done as fast as you can.

**3.** As soon as a Jack is played, you all try to slap it. Whoever slaps it first wins the pile and shuffles it with their own. The player to their left plays a card, and the game continues.

**4.** If you slap a card that isn't a Jack, you have to give a card to whoever played it. If you run out of cards, you have one chance to get back in, by slapping the next Jack. If you don't manage that, you're out.

**5.** The game continues until one player has all the cards.

# Sevens

| Players | 4–14 |
| --- | --- |
| Difficulty | Very easy |
| Deck | 52 cards (use two decks for 8+ players) |
| Goal | To go out first by placing all your cards in a layout |
| Ranks | Aces are low |

In Sevens, you play cards like dominoes.

**1.** Find a large, clear space. Shuffle and deal all the cards.

**2.** The player with the 7 of Diamonds plays it in the middle.

**3.** The next player can play a 6 or 8 to the left or right of the 7, or another 7 above or below it. Take turns to add cards to the left or right, or sevens above or below. Knock the table to pass if you can't. The first out of cards wins.

## Tip

Block other players by holding onto 6s, 7s and 8s for as long as you can.

# James Bond

| | |
|---|---|
| **Players** | 2–3 |
| **Difficulty** | Very easy |
| **Deck** | 52 cards |
| **Goal** | Get four matching cards in all of your piles |

You'll have to be as fast and cunning as a super-spy to win this game where everybody plays at the same time.

**1.** Shuffle the deck. If two people are playing, deal six piles of four cards, face down, to each player. If three play, deal four piles of four cards each.

**2.** Lay out the last four cards in a row, face up, in the middle of the table.

**3.** The dealer says "Go!" and, at the same time, everyone picks up a pile. Each player can swap one card from their pile with any card from the middle, to try and make four matching cards. You can only pick up **one pile at a time,** and you can only swap **one card at a time.**

In the example below, the first pile that one player picks up has two 6s. He swaps one of his 9s for the 6 in the middle, and that pile is nearly complete. Meanwhile, his opponent swaps a 5 for the Jack. He then puts down his pile and takes another, swapping his 3 for the Queen.

**4.** The game continues in a fast and furious fashion until one player has four matching cards in each pile. He then calls out "James Bond!" and everyone turns up their cards.

# Tip

Keep an eye on which cards other players seem to be picking up; if you let go of those cards too soon, it may help them to win before you can.

# Rolling stone

| Players | 3–6 |
|---|---|
| Difficulty | Very easy |
| Deck | 3 players (24 cards): remove cards 2–8 from each suit; 4 players (32 cards): remove cards 2–6; 5 players (40 cards): remove cards 2–4; 6 players (48 cards): remove the 2s |
| Goal | To get rid of all your cards by matching suit |
| Ranks | Aces are high |

The size of your hand changes all the time in this game: just when you think you're winning, you have to pick up.

**1.** Shuffle, and deal eight cards each; none should be left.

**2.** Sort your hands into suit and rank order.

**3.** The player left of the dealer starts by playing any card.

Example of starting hands

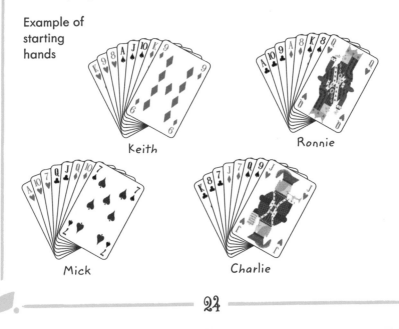

Keith

Ronnie

Mick

Charlie

**4.** You all try to follow suit (play a card of the same suit as the leading card). If everyone has had a turn, and all followed suit, whoever played the highest card wins the round. He puts the cards in the middle aside, then leads the next round with a card from **a different suit to the one just led**, if he can.

**5.** If you can't follow suit, you have to pick up the pile. You must then lead a new round with a card from a different suit to the one just led.

**Example of play**

**1.** Mick leads with the Ace ♥.

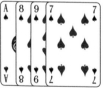

**2.** Keith plays the 8; Ronnie plays the Queen; Charlie plays the Jack.

**3.** Mick won. He discards the cards and leads with the Queen ♣.

**4.** Keith has no Clubs, so he picks up the Queen and leads with the Ace ♠.

**5.** Ronnie plays the 8; Charlie plays the 9; Mick plays the 7.

**6.** Keith won. He discards the cards and leads with the King ♥.

**7.** Ronnie has no Hearts, so he picks up the King and leads a new round...

**6.** The first to run out of cards wins, but be warned, this game can roll on and on...

# Linger longer

| | |
|---|---|
| **Players** | 3–6 |
| **Difficulty** | Very easy |
| **Deck** | 52 cards |
| **Goal** | To be the last player with any cards |
| **Ranks** | Aces are high |

This is a simple game where you try to hold onto your cards for as long as you can.

**1.** Shuffle, then deal ten cards each for three players, seven cards each for four players, six cards for five, or five for six. The dealer shows the last card he dealt himself. The suit of this card will be 'trumps'. Any card in the trump suit beats any card of another suit.

**2.** Put the rest of the cards face down to make a stock pile. Sort your hands by suit and rank.

**3.** The player left of the dealer leads with any card. You must follow suit if you can, otherwise play a trump or any other card.

**Example:** Liv's starting hand

*Sort your hand by suit and rank, like this.*

**4.** The trick is won by the highest card of the leading suit, or by the highest trump if any are played. Keep tricks you win face down in front of you.

**5.** The winner of the trick draws a card from the stock, showing it for the next trumps, and adds it to her hand. She then leads the next trick.

**Example of play** (mid-game)

**1.** Lucy took the last trick, so she draws from the stock. It's the 6♠ so trumps are now Spades. She leads with the King ♥.

**2.** Lewis has no Hearts, so he trumps with the 3♠; Liv plays the 2♥; Liam plays the 3♥.

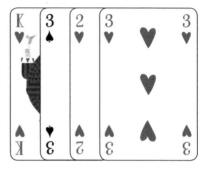

**3.** Lewis's trump wins him the trick. He draws the 9♥ from the stock, so trumps are now Hearts.

**4.** Lewis leads with the Jack ♦; Liv plays the 3; Liam plays the 7; Lucy plays the 10. Lewis wins again.

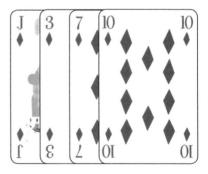

**6.** Players who run out of cards are out. The last player in is the winner. If it comes down to two or more players with a single card left, then whoever takes the last trick wins.

# Stealing bundles

| | |
|---|---|
| **Players** | 2–4 |
| **Difficulty** | Very easy |
| **Deck** | 52 cards |
| **Goal** | To win the most 'bundles' of four matching cards |

In this game you have to 'fish' for matching cards, with the added fun and frustration of stealing each other's wins.

**1.** Everyone picks a card from the deck. Whoever has the highest card deals first. Then take turns to deal, clockwise.

**2.** Deal four cards face down to each player and four cards face up in the middle.

Example of starting hands and table cards

Hannah

Riley

Marc

Olivia

**3.** The player left of the dealer starts. She tries to match a card in her hand to one on the table of the same rank, for example two 5s. If she can, she picks it up and puts the matching cards in a face-up pile in front of her. If there is more than one card of the same rank on the table, she picks them all up. If she can't go, she has to add one of her cards to the table cards.

**4.** You all take turns to do the same, but if you have a card that matches the top card of another player's pile, you can instead steal their whole pile and add it to yours, putting your matching card on top.

**5.** You can also play cards from your hand to your pile if they match the rank of the top card, but you can't just take a card from the table and put it on your pile. If you can't match a table card, steal a pile, or play to your own pile, you must play a card to the table.

**6.** When everyone's hands run out, deal again, but not to the table. When all the cards have been played, sort your pile into rank order. The player with the most sets of four matching cards is the winner.

**Table cards and piles at the end of the first hand**

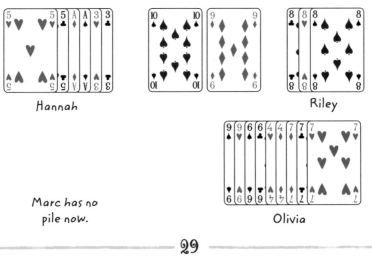

Hannah

Riley

Marc has no
pile now.

Olivia

# President

| | |
|---|---|
| **Players** | 4–7 |
| **Difficulty** | Very easy |
| **Deck** | 54 cards, including two Jokers |
| **Extras** | Paper and pen for scoring |
| **Goal** | To get rid of all your cards as soon as you can |
| **Ranks** | Jokers are high, then 2s, Aces, Kings, and so on |

The first to finish in this game becomes 'President', and each player that follows gets a title of lower rank. At the end of a round, you swap seats to show your new status.

**1.** Deal all the cards. The player left of the dealer leads with any card, or with several cards of the same rank.

**2.** The others try to match or beat the leading cards. For example, if a 9 is played, you can match it with a 9 or beat it with a 10 or higher. If two 9s are laid down, you can match it with two 9s or beat it with two 10s, but not one 10. A single Joker, though, can beat anything.

**3.** Jokers can also be used as wild cards to stand in for any card. For example, 8, 8, Joker would beat 7, 7, 7. But they can then be beaten by any cards higher than those they are standing in for.

**4.** If you can't go, you say "pass." If everyone passes on a card then the pile in the middle is discarded and the leading player goes again.

**5.** The first player to get rid of all her cards becomes President, and the player to her left continues the round. This carries on through as many ranks as you need (see some suggestions on the right). The last to go out is the Citizen, and the one still in is the lowly Dog.

**6.** The **President** scores **two points**, the **Vice-President one**, and the rest score nothing. Swap seats so that the President is sitting in the 'top' chair, with the Vice-President on her left, and so on.

## Ranks

President

Vice-President

Speaker

Senator

Secretary

Citizen

Dog

**7.** The Dog then gathers all the cards, shuffles and deals the next round. Before play, the Dog must give his best card to the President, who then gives him any card she chooses. The game ends when someone reaches ten points.

### Example of play

**1.** Abi plays two 5s.      **2.** Andy plays two 9s.      **3.** Skye passes.

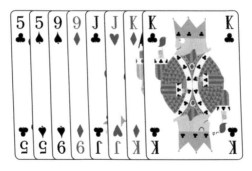

**4.** Dan plays two Jacks.      **5.** Joe passes.      **6.** Max plays two Kings.

# Muggins

| | |
|---|---|
| **Players** | 3–7 |
| **Difficulty** | Very easy |
| **Deck** | 52 cards |
| **Goal** | To be first to get rid of all your cards |
| **Ranks** | Aces are low |

This fast-paced game goes back to the 19th Century.

**1.** If there are three, four or six players, deal four cards face up in the middle. With five players, deal two cards; with seven, deal three. These cards are the **mugginses**.

**2.** Deal the rest of the cards between the players. Don't look at your cards, but make a face-down pile in front of you.

**The start of a game**

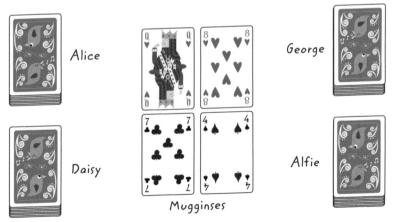

Mugginses

**3.** The player left of the dealer turns up her top card and looks to see if there is a muggins one rank higher or lower to play it on. For example, a 7 could go on any 8 or any 6.

**4.** You can't play Kings on Aces, nor Aces on Kings. If you can't play, you start a face-up discard pile to the left of your face-down pile.

**5.** Take turns clockwise. If you can't play on a muggins, you can play on other players' discard piles in the same way that you would play on a muggins. If your card could go on more than one discard pile, you must play it on the pile of the player nearest your left. If it can't go anywhere, it goes on your discard pile. When your face-down cards run out, turn over your discard pile and start again.

**Example of play**

**1.** Alice turns over a Jack and plays it on the Queen.

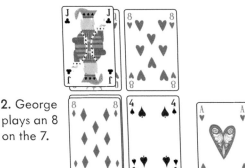

**2.** George plays an 8 on the 7.

**3.** Alfie can't play his 2, so he starts a discard pile.

**4.** Daisy plays an Ace on Alfie's 2.

**6.** If anyone breaks any rules, then everyone calls out "Muggins!" and the other players each give him one card from their pile, which he puts underneath his own. Examples of rule-breaking include playing on a card that isn't one rank higher or lower, or playing on someone's discard pile when you could have played on a muggins.

**7.** The next player then continues. First out of cards wins.

# Snip Snap Snorum

| | |
|---|---|
| Players | 4–8 |
| Difficulty | Very easy |
| Deck | 52 cards |
| Goal | To get rid of all your cards |
| Ranks | Aces are low |

This old game is all about playing cards in sequence.

**1.** Deal all the cards among the players. Sort your hands by suit and rank.

**2.** The player left of the dealer starts by playing any card, calling "Snip!"

**3.** The player with the next card above it in the same suit plays it on top (such as the 7♣ on the 6♣) calling "Snap!"

**4.** The player of the next card calls "Snorum!", the next "Hi-cockalorum!" and the next "Jig!" The caller of Jig ends the sequence, and plays a new card, calling "Snip!"

Finley

Mia

Matt plays the 10, Jack and Queen ♠, calling Snip, Snap, Snorum!

Leoni

Matt

**5.** A sequence may stop when you reach a King or a card that has already been played. When that happens, and no one can go, no matter where you are in the sequence whoever played the last card calls "Jig!" then starts a new sequence with "Snip!"

**6.** The first player out of cards is the winner. The dealer moves to the left for the next game.

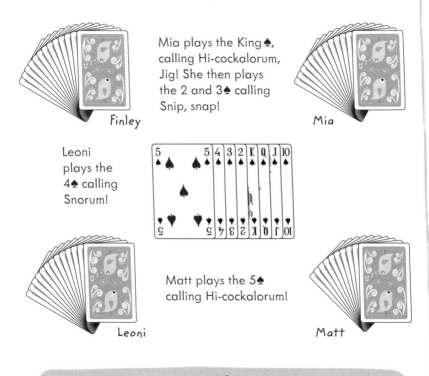

Mia plays the King ♠, calling Hi-cockalorum, Jig! She then plays the 2 and 3♠ calling Snip, snap!

Finley

Mia

Leoni plays the 4♠ calling Snorum!

Matt plays the 5♠ calling Hi-cockalorum!

Leoni

Matt

# Tip

When you get to lead, if you can't play a sequence of cards, see if you have two cards in one suit that are five ranks apart. Playing the first of them will get you to Jig and give you the lead again.

# Ten-Ten-Five-One

| | |
|---|---|
| **Players** | 2 |
| **Difficulty** | Easy |
| **Deck** | 52 cards |
| **Goal** | To win the most tricks |
| **Ranks** | Aces are high |

This is a simple game similar to **whist** (see page 62). The name of the game tells you how to deal the cards.

1. First deal a line of ten cards face down to each player.

2. Deal ten cards face up on top of those.

3. Deal five cards each as a hand.

4. Deal one 'mystery card' each, face down.

Sam's cards

Sam's mystery card

Simon's mystery card

Sam's hand

Simon's hand

Simon's cards

**5.** The non-dealer plays first, using any card from his hand, any of his face-up cards, or his unseen mystery card. If you play a face-up card, you then turn up the face-down card underneath it. You can't look at your mystery card before deciding to play it.

**6.** The next player must follow suit if he can. The player of the highest card wins the trick. The winner leads the next trick. Store your tricks in a pile face down next to you.

1. Simon plays the King ♥ and turns up the Ace ♣.

2. Sam sees he can't win this trick, so he plays his lowest Heart, the 4♥ and turns up the 10♥.

**3.** Simon now knows that Sam doesn't have the Ace ♥, so he plays the Queen ♥. Sam plays the 7♥ and Simon takes his second trick.

**7.** When all the cards have been played and the last trick taken, count your cards to see who won most tricks.

# Tip

By working out what cards your opponent has, you can guess their weakest suits.

# Golf

| Players | 2–8 |
|---|---|
| Difficulty | Easy |
| Deck | 2–4 players: 52 cards; 5–8 players: use two decks |
| Extras | Paper and pen to keep score |
| Goal | To reach the lowest score by making pairs |
| Values | Queens, Jacks and 10s: +10; Aces: +1; Kings: 0; 2s: –2; Other number cards: face value |

As in the sport, the goal of this card game is to end with the lowest score.

**1.** Deal six cards to each player. Place the rest in the middle to make a stock pile, then turn over the top card to start a discard pile.

**2.** Arrange your cards in front of you, face down, in a two-by-three grid. Pick two cards, without looking at them, and turn them face up in the grid.

**3.** The point of the game is to end up with the lowest possible grid cards. Any matching vertical pair of cards, including 2s, scores 0.

**4.** The player left of the dealer starts. She can either draw a card from the stock or the top of the discard pile, or use her turn to turn one of her grid cards face up.

Lay out your cards in a two-by-three grid.

**5.** If she takes a card from the discard pile, she must use it to replace one of her grid cards. If she replaces a face-down card, she can't look at it first.

**6.** If she draws a card from the stock, she can discard it, or she can use it to replace a card in her grid.

**7.** Play continues clockwise until one player turns up the last card in their grid, then all scores are counted. The player with the lowest score after nine rounds wins.

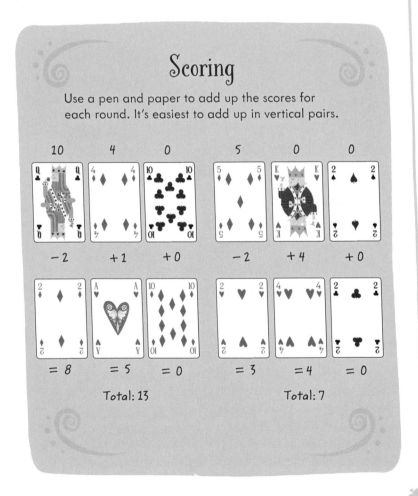

# Scoring

Use a pen and paper to add up the scores for each round. It's easiest to add up in vertical pairs.

| 10 | 4 | 0 | 5 | 0 | 0 |
|----|----|----|----|----|----|
| − 2 | + 1 | + 0 | − 2 | + 4 | + 0 |
| = 8 | = 5 | = 0 | = 3 | = 4 | = 0 |

Total: 13          Total: 7

# Thirteens

| Players | 1 |
|---|---|
| Difficulty | Easy |
| Deck | 48 cards (remove the Kings) |
| Goal | To discard the cards in pairs adding up to 13 |
| Values | Queen: 12; Jack: 11; Ace: 1; number cards: face value |

**Patience** or **solitaire** games are games for a single player. This one is all about adding up to 13.

**1.** Shuffle the cards and lay five cards face up in a row. Discard any pairs that add up to 13 (see **Values** above). For example, 7+6, Queen+Ace, Jack+2.

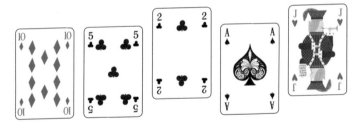

**2.** When no more pairs can be removed, deal another five cards across the remaining cards and gaps. Some cards will now be piled up.

**3.** Continue to discard pairs, using only the top cards of the piles. When you have a gap, fill it with the top card from another pile. When no more pairs can be removed, deal another five cards across the piles, and so on.

**4.** You win if you discard all the cards. It helps if you can remember which cards are at the bottom of the piles.

# Bristol solitaire

| | |
|---|---|
| **Players** | 1 |
| **Difficulty** | Easy |
| **Deck** | 52 cards |
| **Goal** | To place all the cards in four 'foundation' piles from Ace up to King, ignoring suits |

Bristol is easier to win than many solitaires, but think ahead.

**1.** Shuffle the cards and lay them out as illustrated, in eight fans of three cards, with three cards face up below to start waste piles. Leave space above for the foundations.

**2.** If any fans have Kings, put the Kings underneath (see picture). The rest of the cards make the stock.

Foundations

**3.** You play with the top cards of the fans and waste piles. Start by moving any available Aces to start foundations.

**4.** Play cards one at a time to foundations, going up one in rank, or to fans, going down one in rank.

Stock    Waste piles

**5.** You can't move cards to waste piles, or from foundations. When you can't go, deal three more cards across the waste piles and continue playing. You win when all the foundations have been built up from Ace to King.

# Martha patience

| | |
|---|---|
| **Players** | 1 |
| **Difficulty** | Easy |
| **Deck** | 52 cards |
| **Goal** | To sort all the cards into suits, on four foundations |

In Martha patience, half the cards are hidden at the start.

**1.** Lay the four Aces out to make 'foundation' piles. Shuffle the other cards and lay them out in four overlapping rows of 12, making 12 columns of four cards:

**2.** You can use any of the face-up cards at the bottom of the columns. Start by moving any free 2s onto the Ace of the same suit, then any 3s, and so on. When you uncover a face-down card, turn it face up. You can use it now.

**3.** You can uncover more cards by moving face-up cards to another column. They have to go down by one rank, and alternating red and black suits. So you could move a red 5 onto a black 6, for example, then a black 4 onto the 5. You can move sequences of cards too, but if you empty a whole column you can only restart it with a single card.

**4.** You win the game if you manage to put all the cards onto the foundations, ending with the four Kings.

# Catch the Ten

| | |
|---|---|
| **Players** | 2–8 playing singly or in teams |
| **Difficulty** | Easy |
| **Deck** | 2, 3, 4 or 6 players: 36 cards (remove cards 2–5 from each suit); 5 or 7 players: 35 cards (remove cards 2–6); 8 players: 40 cards (remove cards 2–4). |
| **Extras** | Paper and pen to keep score |
| **Goal** | To win tricks and top trumps |
| **Ranks** | Aces are high |
| **Top trumps** | Ace: 11; King: 4; Queen: 3; Jack: 2; Ten: 10 |

The goal of this whist-like game is to win the top trumps in tricks, especially the Ten, which can be taken by all the other top trumps but is worth a lot.

**1.** Deal all the cards. Show the last one dealt. That suit will be trumps. If two people are playing, deal three six-card hands each; with three, deal two hands each. You must play out each hand before you pick up the next.

**2.** The player left of the dealer leads with any card. You must follow suit if you can, but if you can't you can play what you like. The highest card of the leading suit wins, or the highest trump if any are played. Keep tricks in a pile face down in front of you. The winner of each trick leads the next.

**3.** After each hand, score for any top trumps you won then add one point for each card you won *minus* the number of cards you were dealt at the start of the game.

**4.** The winner of the last hand leads. First to **41 points** wins.

# Chinese Ten

| | |
|---|---|
| Players | 2–4 |
| Difficulty | Easy |
| Deck | 52 cards |
| Goal | To score points by winning cards from the table |

In this Chinese game you win red cards and high-value black Aces by adding up card values to make ten.

**1.** Deal 12 cards each for two players, eight each for three, or six each for four. Deal the next four cards face up on the table around the remaining deck, which makes a stock pile. If two or more are the same rank (for example, two Jacks) bury them in the deck and deal another four.

**2.** The player left of the dealer starts, trying to win a card by making ten. **Aces equal one.** So, for example, an Ace wins a 9, a 9 wins an Ace, or a 3 a 7. But **10s and picture cards can only be won by cards of the same rank.**

Stock

**3.** If you win a card, put the two cards in a face-down pile in front of you. If you can't, or don't want to because you can't win anything of value, add a card in a free space on the table. Either way, you lose one card each turn.

**Example of play**

A King wins a King.          A 4 wins a 6.

**4.** At the end of your turn, turn up the top card of the stock. If it can win any of the table cards, you add the cards to your pile. If it can't, you add it to the table.

**5.** If you play without making any mistakes, the last card of the stock will win the last table card. Add up your scores to find the winner.

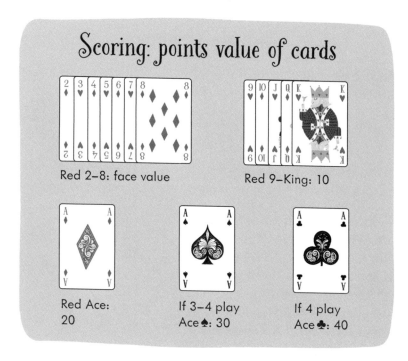

# Scoring: points value of cards

Red 2–8: face value          Red 9–King: 10

Red Ace:     If 3–4 play     If 4 play
20           Ace ♠: 30       Ace ♣: 40

# Rummy

| | |
|---|---|
| **Players** | 2–6 |
| **Difficulty** | Easy |
| **Deck** | 52 cards (Jokers are optional as wild cards) |
| **Extras** | (Classic rummy only) paper and pen for scoring |
| **Goal** | To make sequences and matching sets |
| **Ranks** | Aces are low |
| **Values** | (Classic rummy only) Picture cards: 10; Aces: 1; number cards: face value; Jokers: 0 |

Rummy is a very popular game with many versions. These rules are for a simple version and the classic game. The rules for **gin rummy** are on page 74.

## Simple rummy

**1.** Choose a dealer for the first round. With two players, the winner deals the next round. With more, take turns.

**2.** Shuffle well, then deal seven cards each for 2–4 players or six cards each for 5–6 players.

**3.** Put the rest of the cards face down in the middle to make a stock pile and turn over a card to make a discard pile.

**4.** Sort your hand by suit and rank. You aim to pick up cards that let you build up a hand of **sets** (groups of three or four cards of the same rank) and **runs** (sequences of three or four cards of the same suit). A hand can be all sets, all runs, or contain both.

A complete hand

**5.** Each turn goes like this: **Draw a card** from either the stock or the top of the discard pile, add it to your hand, then **discard a card.** If your card came from the discard pile, you can't discard it in the same turn.

**6.** When, after discarding a card, your hand is complete with both a three-card and a four-card group, you call "Rummy!" and lay it down. You win that round.

**Example of play**

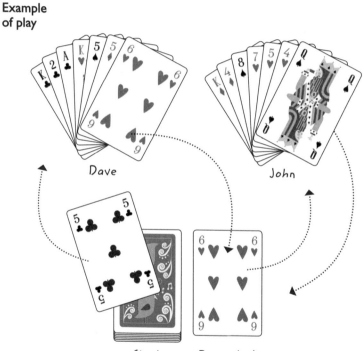

Stock          Discard pile

Dave draws the 5♣ from the stock. He discards his 6♥. He now has a set of three 5s.

John picks up the 6♥ from the discard pile and discards his Queen. He now has a 4-card run.

**7.** The game ends when an agreed number of rounds are played. Whoever wins the most rounds wins the game.

# Classic rummy

In classic rummy, the object is to get rid of all your cards. For two players, you deal ten cards. For more, deal the same as **simple rummy** (page 46).

**1.** Unlike simple rummy, on your turn, after drawing a card, you can **meld** (lay on the table) one set or run (see page 46).

**2.** After melding, you can **lay off** cards. This means adding cards from your hand to melds on the table, to complete a set or extend a run (in this version, a run can be more than four cards). After either, you must still discard a card. With two players, you can only add to your own melds; with more, you can add to any meld on the table.

**Example of melding**

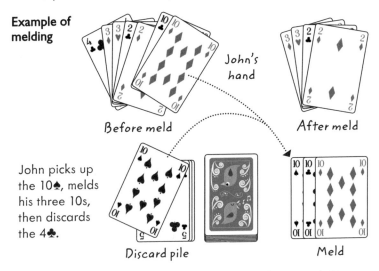

John's hand

Before meld

After meld

John picks up the 10♠, melds his three 10s, then discards the 4♣.

Discard pile

Meld

**3.** You win a round when you play your last card. You score points for the cards the other players still have in their hands (see **Values** on page 46). The game ends when one player gets **100 points** (or any score you agree). If you finish all at once without melding or laying off cards in a previous turn, you have 'gone rummy', and score double points.

# Cucumber

| | |
|---|---|
| Players | 2–8 |
| Difficulty | Easy |
| Deck | 52 cards |
| Extras | Paper and pen to keep score |
| Goal | Not to be left with the highest card |
| Ranks | Aces are high |
| Penalties | Ace: 14; King: 13; Queen: 12; Jack: 11; number cards: face value |

In this Swedish game, you try to ensure that the one card you have left after the fifth trick is not the highest in play, or it will score you penalty points.

**1.** Deal six cards each. The player left of the dealer leads with any card he likes.

**2.** You take turns trying to play a card of equal or higher rank to the last card played – suits don't matter. If you can't equal it or beat it, **you must play your lowest card** – this is a vital rule, as the game is all about holding on to low cards.

**3.** Whoever played the highest card takes the trick and puts it aside. For equal cards, the last played wins.

**4.** The winner leads the next trick. After five tricks have been played, everyone shows their last card and the player or players with the highest cards receive penalty points (see **Penalties** above). Whoever reaches **30 penalty points** is 'cucumbered' (knocked out). The last to stay in wins.

**Tip**

Hold on to a high card for later rounds, so you aren't forced to play your lowest.

# Jubilee

| Players | 2–7 |
|---|---|
| Difficulty | Easy |
| Deck | 61 cards, made out of two 54-card decks like this: 2 Clubs suits without the 10s or picture cards + 2 Spades suits + 1 Hearts suit + 4 Jokers |
| Extras | Paper and pen to keep score |
| Goal | To score points by making 'jubilees' (multiples of 25) |
| Values | Ace: 15; picture card: 10; number cards: face value; Joker: 0; **Hearts subtract** from the total |

This Czech counting game is all about multiples of 25.

**1.** Deal eight cards each. Put the rest face down as a stock. Order your hands by value (see above).

**2.** The player left of the dealer starts by playing a black card face up in the middle; if he has none, the player to his left starts. After you play, draw a new card from the stock, if there is one.

**3.** You can follow with any card, calling out the new total of the face-up pile, but you can't bring the total below zero (Hearts are negative). If you can't go, show your hand to the other players and pass.

You can't play a Heart that would bring the total below zero.

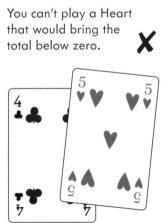

**4.** When you play a card that brings the total to 25, or a multiple (50, 75, etc.) you score **10 points.** When the total is also a multiple of 100, you **score 20 points.** But if you 'jump a jubilee', going up or going down, you **lose 5 points.**

For example, if the total is 20 and you play the 6♠, the total goes up to 26, jumping a jubilee. Or if the total is 30 and you play the 6♥, it falls to 24, jumping a jubilee downwards. Keep score as you go.

**5.** Jokers are worth 0, so playing one just after a jubilee means that you score a jubilee too. Continue until all the cards are played, and the highest scorer wins.

Example (mid-play)

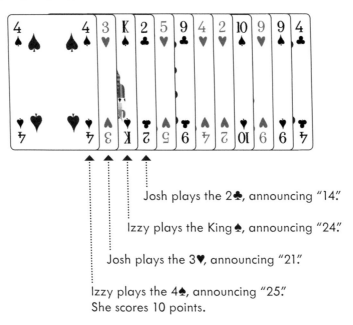

Josh plays the 2♣, announcing "14."

Izzy plays the King ♠, announcing "24."

Josh plays the 3♥, announcing "21."

Izzy plays the 4♠, announcing "25." She scores 10 points.

# Thirty-one

| | |
|---|---|
| **Players** | 2–9 |
| **Difficulty** | Easy |
| **Deck** | 52 cards |
| **Extras** | 3 life counters per player (see page 110 for ideas) |
| **Goal** | To collect cards in one suit worth 31 points, or as close to 31 as possible |
| **Values** | Aces: 11; Picture cards: 10; number cards: face value |

In this game, you battle to be the first to make 31 points.

**1.** Choose a dealer. Shuffle, and deal three cards each. Each player also gets three counters to stand for lives.

**2.** Put the rest of the cards in the middle to make a stock pile, and turn a card face up to start a discard pile.

**3.** The player left of the dealer draws the top card of the stock or discard pile. He then discards a card (but you can't discard a card you've just picked up from the discard pile).

**4.** At the start of your turn, if you think your hand is good enough you can knock on the table instead of playing. Anyone yet to play takes their turn, then you all add up your cards to find your scores (see **Scoring** opposite).

**5.** If you reach exactly **31 points** you can call it at any time, and the rest lose, each placing a life counter in the middle, even if they've knocked.

*You need an Ace, worth 11, to make a hand of 31 points.*

# Scoring

You find the best score you can make with your hand using cards of only one suit (see **Values** on page 52). For example:

27 points for all three

13 points for the 9 and 4

11 points for the Ace

# Tip

Watch closely to see what suits others are picking up: they can't make 31 if you have the Ace in their suit.

**6.** The player with the lowest-scoring hand loses a life, placing one of her counters in the middle. If a player who knocked has the lowest hand, he loses two lives. If there's a tie for lowest place, all the tied players lose a life unless one is the knocker, in which case he keeps it.

**7.** Players who lose their last life keep on playing, but as soon as they have the lowest hand again, they are out for good. The last player in is the winner.

# Crazy Eights

| Players | 2+ |
|---|---|
| Difficulty | Easy |
| Deck | 52 cards (for 7+ players, use two decks) |
| Goal | To get rid of all your cards |

Like **Egyptian rat slap** (page 58), this is great for a crowd. Having to remember all the special cards is part of the fun.

**1.** Shuffle the cards and deal five cards each, or seven each if just two are playing. Sort your hands by rank.

**2.** Place the rest of the cards face down in the middle to make a stock pile. Turn the top card face up to start a discard pile. If it's an 8, bury it in the stock and turn over another.

**3.** The player left of the dealer plays on the discard pile a card that follows suit, or any number of cards that match its rank. You can also play an 8, but it's best to save those until you really need them. See opposite for the effects of playing 8s and other **special cards**.

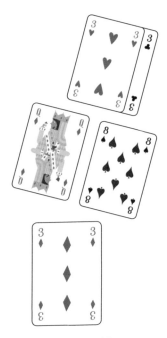

**4.** If you can't play, or don't want to, you draw a card from the stock.

On a 3♦ you could play any number of 3s, any Diamond, or an 8.

**5.** When you know you can get rid of all your cards on your next turn, you must declare "last card(s)." If you play your last card but have forgotten to declare, you have to pick up two cards.

**6.** If the stock runs out, shuffle all but the top card of the discard pile well to make a new stock. The first player to get rid of all his cards wins.

# Special cards

Here's what happens when you play these cards:

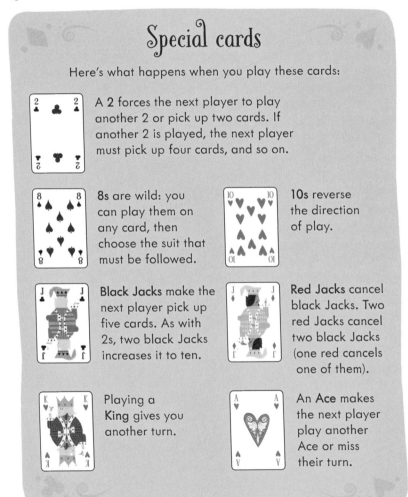

A **2** forces the next player to play another 2 or pick up two cards. If another 2 is played, the next player must pick up four cards, and so on.

**8s** are wild: you can play them on any card, then choose the suit that must be followed.

**10s** reverse the direction of play.

**Black Jacks** make the next player pick up five cards. As with 2s, two black Jacks increases it to ten.

**Red Jacks** cancel black Jacks. Two red Jacks cancel two black Jacks (one red cancels one of them).

Playing a **King** gives you another turn.

An **Ace** makes the next player play another Ace or miss their turn.

# Kings' corners

| | |
|---|---|
| Players | 2+ |
| Difficulty | Easy |
| Deck | 52 cards (with 7+ players, use two decks) |
| Goal | To empty your hand by playing to a layout |
| Ranks | Aces are low |

This game of competitive patience is simple but addictive.

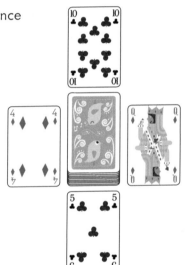

**1.** Deal seven cards each. Put the rest face down to make a stock pile. Turn up four cards around it at north, east, south and west. If there are more than two Aces showing, shuffle the four cards into the stock and turn up four more.

**2.** The player left of the dealer plays in as many of these four ways as she can or wants to:

- **Play a card on any pile,** going down one in rank, and alternating red and black suits; for example, the 10♣ on the Jack♥. Leave the bottom card of the pile sticking out slightly, so its rank can be seen. Aces are low, so you can't play on them.

- **Move a whole pile** onto another if its bottom card is a rank lower than the other pile's top card **and** the red and black suits alternate.

- **Play a King into a corner space** (see below) or move a whole pile with a King at the bottom into a corner space. (If playing with two decks, a completed King-Ace pile can be removed and replaced with a new King or a new King pile.)

- **Play any card** from your hand to an empty north, south, east or west space.

**3.** She then **takes a card from the stock** and the next player takes his turn. When a player empties her hand, she has won. The cards are shuffled and dealt by the player left of the last dealer, and the next game begins.

**4.** When the stock runs out, play on without drawing more cards.

**5.** You can decide that whoever wins the most of, say, three or five games wins. Or you can award players penalty points for each card left in their hands when somebody wins (10 for a King, 1 for other cards). When one player reaches 25, then the player with fewest penalty points wins.

**At the end of a game**

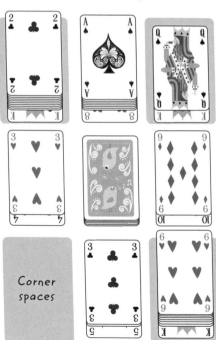

Corner spaces

# Egyptian rat slap

| | |
|---|---|
| **Players** | 2+ |
| **Difficulty** | Easy |
| **Deck** | 54 cards, including two Jokers (for 9+ players, combine two 54-card decks) |
| **Goal** | To win all the cards |

This fast, funny game involves slapping cards, paying penalties and plenty of other twists.

**1.** Shuffle the cards and deal them equally, putting any left-over cards face up in a central pile.

**2.** Place your cards face down in a pile in front of you. Take turns turning over the top card of your pile onto the central pile. You can't look at your own cards before everyone else (as in **Snap** on page 6).

**3.** If a number card is played, the next player takes her turn. If an **Ace** is played, the next player must play **four cards** (another Ace or a picture card being turned up stops the turn **immediately**, and the next person must play). If four number cards are played, the player of the Ace wins the pile, puts it under his own, then plays again. Picture cards also have this rule, but you have to play different numbers of cards.

Ace: 4 cards

King: 3 cards

Queen: 2 cards

Jack: 1 card

**4.** Players can also win the pile by slapping their hand down on it when certain cards come up – see below.

**5.** If you slap the pile incorrectly, you have to add two cards from your pile to the bottom of the central pile.

**6.** If you lose all your cards, you are out of the game, but you can still get back in by slapping the cards.

**7.** The game ends when one player has all the cards.

# Slappable cards

These combinations can be slapped:

**Pair** Two matching cards

**Sandwich** Two matching cards separated by another card

**Four in a row** A sequence of four cards, ignoring suits

**Bottoms up** The top card of the pile is the same rank as the bottom card.

**Marriage** A King and Queen

**Joker** A Joker can always be slapped.

# Racing demon

| | |
|---|---|
| **Players** | 2+ |
| **Difficulty** | Easy |
| **Deck** | One 52-card deck per player, each with a different back |
| **Goal** | To get rid of all the cards in your 'demon' pile, and to get as many of your cards into the shared foundation piles as you can. |

This fast and furious race game is great with lots of players.

**1.** Each player shuffles then deals a face-down 'demon' pile of 13 cards, with the top card turned face up.

**2.** You then deal a row of four cards, face up, to make work piles. The remaining cards, face down, become a stock pile.

**3.** You all play at the same time, turning over three cards from your stock to start a discard pile. You always turn over cards from the stock three at a time.

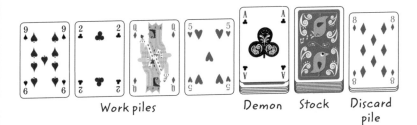

Work piles                              Demon    Stock    Discard
                                                           pile

**4.** You play by placing cards on your work piles going down one in rank, red then black, like this: 8♥ on 9♠. You can also move cards, or card sequences, between work piles. You can play with the top card of your demon or of your discard pile. After you play from your demon, turn the next card face up.

**5.** Put any Ace you find in the middle. Anyone can use it to build that suit from Ace up to King. If you clash when trying to play a card on a middle pile ('foundation') the fastest wins, and losers return their cards to where they came from.

   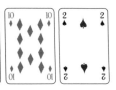

Steve

Steve can play the 9♣ on the 10♦ and the Ace ♥ into the middle.

Lewis can play the 8♦ on the 9♠, then the Ace ♣ into the middle and the 2♣ on that.

Lewis

**6.** Restart empty work piles with a stock or demon card.

**7.** When you can't turn over another three cards because there are too few in your stock, place them on the discard pile and turn it over to make a new stock.

**8.** If everyone gets stuck, make new stocks by all turning over your discard piles, placing the top card underneath.

**9.** When you have emptied your demon and think you have a good number of cards built up in the foundations, you can call out "Demon!" and the game ends.

**10.** After a game, you **score 1 point** for each of your cards in a **foundation**, and **lose 2 points** for each card left in your **demon**. You can tell whose cards are whose by the different backs. Play until someone wins by reaching 100 points.

# Knockout whist

| | |
|---|---|
| Players | 3–7 |
| Difficulty | Easy |
| Deck | 52 cards |
| Goal | To stay in by winning tricks with high cards and trumps |
| Ranks | Aces are high |

There are many games called 'whist' where you try to win the most tricks – this is a fun and simple version.

1. Deal seven cards each. Put the rest in a pile, turning over the top one to show the trump suit for the first round.

2. Sort your hands by suit and rank. The player left of the dealer plays any card face up. Each player must then try to play a higher card. You must follow suit if you can. If you can't, you can play a trump or any other card. The highest card of the leading suit wins, or the highest trump if any are played. You keep tricks you win in face-down piles.

If Clubs were trumps, this trick would be won by the player of the 2♣. If Diamonds were trumps, the 6♦ would win. If Hearts or Spades were trumps, the player of the Ace♥ would take the trick.

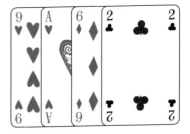

3. The winner of each trick leads the next one. When everyone has played their hand, whoever has taken the most tricks wins the round. Anyone who takes no tricks is knocked out.

**4.** The player left of the dealer deals next, shuffling and dealing six cards each. The winner of the last round picks trumps. If there was a tie, draw cards and the highest wins.

**5.** Each round is then played with one less card. Just one card each is dealt in the seventh round, if you get that far. The last player in, or whoever takes the last trick, wins.

**Example of play:** 5th round
(trumps are Diamonds)

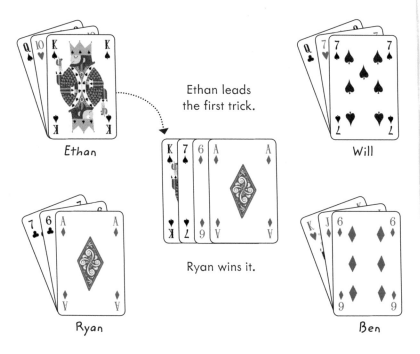

Ethan

Ethan leads
the first trick.

Will

Ryan

Ryan wins it.

Ben

**6.** If you like, you can give players who win no tricks in a round two more 'lives' before they are knocked out. First you are a 'dog' and are dealt just one card in the next round. You can choose which trick to play in, and, if you win it, are dealt back into the game. If you fail, you then get a last chance as a 'blind dog' and are dealt one card face down, which you must play without looking at it.

# Oh well!

| | |
|---|---|
| Players | 3–7 |
| Difficulty | Easy |
| Deck | 52 cards |
| Extras | Paper and pen to keep score |
| Goal | To win the number of tricks that you bid |
| Ranks | Aces are high |

Known by many names, this whist-like game is all about predicting the exact number of tricks you will win.

**1.** Choose one person to be scorekeeper and another to be the first dealer. The scorekeeper makes a scoresheet with one column for each player.

**2.** Deal ten cards each for 3–5 players, eight cards each for six players, or seven cards each for seven. Put the rest aside, turning up one for trumps.

| Meg | Lucas | Carly |
|---|---|---|
| 7 | 4 | 12 |
| 4 | 4 | 12 24 |
| 2 | 12 | 2 |
| 4 | 11 23 | 13 37 |

**3.** Study your cards to work out how many tricks you think you can win in the round. The player left of the dealer is the first to make his bid, which can be anything from none to the full number of cards dealt that round.

**4.** The total number of tricks bid by all the players is not allowed to be the same as the total number of tricks to be won. The dealer can be at a disadvantage, as he bids last.

**5.** As the players take turns to make their bids, the scorekeeper notes them down at the top of their columns.

**6.** The player left of the dealer leads the first trick. Take turns clockwise. You must follow suit if you can, otherwise you can play anything. The highest card of the leading suit wins the trick, or the highest trump if any are played. The winner of the trick leads the next, and so on.

**Example of play:** 8th round (trumps are Spades)

Meg bids
1 trick.

Lucas bids
1 trick.

Carly bids
0 tricks.

Meg leads the first
trick, Lucas wins it.

Lucas leads the next
trick. Meg wins.

Meg leads the last
trick. Lucas wins.

**7.** At the end of each round, those who took the number of tricks they bid score that number **plus ten**. Those who failed to take the exact number they bid score **nothing**. So in our example above Meg scores 11, Lucas scores 0, and Carly scores 10. The scorekeeper can cross out failed bids to make the adding up easier at the end.

**8.** The dealer moves left. Each round is dealt with one less card, the last round having single-card hands, so the number of rounds is the same as the number of cards dealt in the first round. The player with most points at the end wins.

# Garbage

| | |
|---|---|
| **Players** | 3–8 |
| **Difficulty** | Easy |
| **Deck** | 52 cards (4–5 players: 2 decks; 6–8 players: 3 decks) |
| **Extras** | 50 counters per player (see page 110 for ideas) |
| **Goal** | To win the most counters |
| **Values** | Ace: 1; number cards: face value; Jack: 11; Queen: 12; King: 13 |

'Garbage' combines four short games of luck.

**1. Poker** You all put an agreed amount in the pot, for example, five counters. Choose the first dealer. Deal five cards each, face up. Leave the rest face down in the deck. The player with the best poker hand (see page 95) wins the pot. In our example, Oscar wins with a pair of 6s. In a tie, the pot is split equally between the winners, any left-over counters going to the dealer.

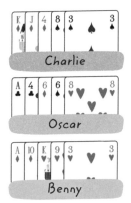

**2. Bingo** Line up your Poker cards in front of you. The dealer turns up cards from the deck one by one, calling their ranks, for example "Ace." If you have any, put a counter on each one every time it's called. The first with all five cards covered by counters wins all the counters on all the cards. In a tie, split the counters as before.

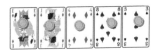

**3. Pay and win** All but the dealer keep their cards. He shuffles the unused deck with his cards and the cards he turned up for Bingo. He then turns up cards from the deck, one by one, calling them. If you have that rank you **pay** into the pot. If he calls "One is 6" and you have any 6s, pay a counter for each. For the second card ("Two is Jack") you pay two, and so on up to the tenth card, worth ten counters.

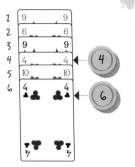

Charlie has a 4. He pays four for the 4th card and six for the 6th.

The dealer turns up ten more cards. This time, if you have any cards you **win** a counter from the pot for each, and so on up to the tenth card, worth ten. If there are still counters in the pot after the tenth card, the dealer wins them. But if the pot has run out, the dealer has to pay the winners himself.

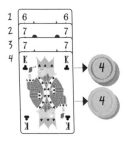

Charlie and Benny have Kings. They take four for the 4th card.

**4. The count-up** The dealer shuffles all the cards with the unused deck, then turns up cards one by one, counting up once through the ranks from Ace to King. If any cards happen to match the rank he's calling, you all pay him their value. If no cards match, the dealer has to pay all the other players five counters each.

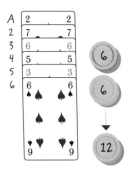

**5.** After the count-up, the dealer moves clockwise. Play again until you've all dealt once, or twice. If anyone runs out of counters they're out. Whoever finishes with most counters wins.

Charlie and Benny pay Oscar six counters each.

# Stops

| | |
|---|---|
| **Players** | 3–8 |
| **Difficulty** | Easy |
| **Deck** | 52 cards + the Jack♠, Queen♦, King♣ and Ace♥ from any other deck (the 'pay cards') |
| **Extras** | 25 counters per player (see page 110 for ideas) |
| **Goal** | To get rid of your cards first, and win counters |
| **Ranks** | Aces are high |

This fun betting game is also called **Michigan** or **Newmarket**.

**1.** Pick a dealer. She lays out the four **pay cards** in the middle, then puts two counters on each card. The other players put one on each. The dealer shuffles the cards and deals the whole deck out among the players, plus an extra 'dummy' hand which is left face down and unused.

**2.** Sort your cards by suit and rank. The player on the dealer's left plays his lowest card face up in front of him, for example, the 3♣. If he has the next card in that suit (4♣) he plays it on top. If he doesn't have it, whoever does plays it, and so on.

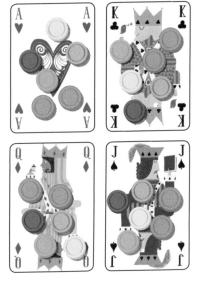

*The pay cards*

**3.** If no one can play the next card because it's already been played, it's in the dummy hand, or an Ace has just been played (the highest in a suit), he leads with his lowest card of **another suit**. If he has no other, the player on his left leads.

**4.** If someone plays a card that matches a pay card, they win all the counters on that card. If no one does, it remains until the next game, and more counters are added to it.

**5.** The first player to run out of cards wins the game and gets one counter from the others for each card left in their hands.

**6.** If a player runs out of counters, he is out. Play enough games for everyone to deal once or twice, then whoever has the most counters wins.

### Example of play
(mid-game)

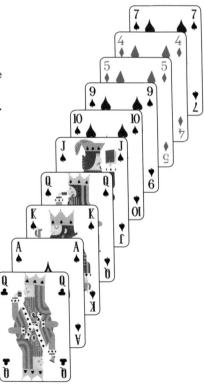

**1.** Louie plays the 7♠; no one has the 8, so he leads with the 4 and 5♦; no one has the 6♦, so he leads again with the 9♠.

**2.** Katie plays the 10♠.

**3.** Frankie plays the Jack ♠ and wins the counters on its pay card.

**4.** Billy plays the Queen.

**5.** Frankie plays the King.

**6.** Billy plays the Ace ♠ then wins the game by playing his last card, the Queen ♣.

# Pip-pip!

| | |
|---|---|
| Players | 4–8 |
| Difficulty | Easy |
| Deck | 104 cards (two 52-card decks) |
| Extras | Paper and pen for scoring |
| Goal | To win valuable cards, and score for changing trumps |
| Ranks | 2s are high, followed by Aces, Kings, and so on |
| Values | 2: 11; Ace: 10; King: 5; Queen: 4; Jack: 3; other cards: 0 |

In this lively game from the 1920s, you try to win valuable cards, and change trumps by matching a King and Queen.

**1.** Deal seven cards each. Place the rest face down to make a stock pile. Turn over the top card to show the trumps suit, half-covering it with the stock.

**2.** The player left of the dealer leads, playing any card face up on the table.

**Tom's hand**
(mid-game)

**3.** You all follow suit if you can; if not, you can play anything. The highest card of the leading suit wins the trick, or the highest trump if any are played. For identical cards, the last played wins. The winner draws a card from the stock, followed by all the other players, then leads the next trick.

Tom plans to use his King and Queen to change trumps to Spades.

**4.** If at any time you have both the **King and Queen** of one suit that isn't the trump suit, you can call "**Pip-pip!**" and lay them in front of you. This scores you **50 points** and trumps change to that suit in the next trick (not the current one). If another pip-pip is declared in the same trick, it also scores, and trumps will change to that suit instead.

**Example of play** (trumps are Clubs)

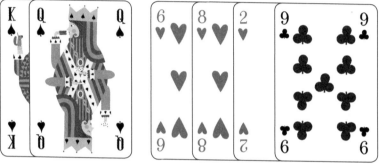

Tom's pip-pip        Chloe   Zoe   Harry   Tom

Tom plays a pip-pip, which will change trumps to Spades in the following trick. Chloe leads with a Heart. Tom has no Hearts, so he plays a trump to take the trick.

**5.** Although pip-pip cards lie in front of you, you can still play them normally – but not to score another pip-pip.

**6.** When the stock runs out, keep on playing without drawing new cards. Not all players may be able to play the last trick.

**7.** When all the cards have been played, everyone looks at their tricks and adds up their score. If you want to play several games, you could play enough for everyone to deal once, then find the overall winner.

# Commerce

| | |
|---|---|
| **Players** | 3–12 |
| **Difficulty** | Easy |
| **Deck** | 52 cards |
| **Extras** | Three counters per player (see page 110 for ideas) |
| **Goal** | To make the best hand and win the pot |
| **Ranks** | Aces are high; in a run, Aces may be high or low but not both |
| **Values** | Ace: 11; picture card: 10; number card: face value |

In this old French game, you try to make the best three-card hand you can.

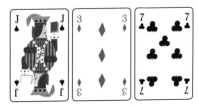

Widow hand

**1.** Everyone pays one counter into the pot.

**2.** Choose a dealer randomly. Deal three cards face down to each player plus an extra 'widow' hand face up in the middle. Before the dealer looks at her hand, she can choose to swap her hand with the widow if she wants.

**3.** The player **right** of the dealer goes first. He swaps any one of his cards for a widow card if it will improve his hand (see page 73). Continue playing to the **right**. When you think you can't improve your hand any more, knock on the table. Once you've knocked you can't swap again, so pass if you need to.

**4.** When two players have knocked, the game ends and you all show your cards. The best hand wins the pot. In a tie, cut the deck and the highest card wins.

# Commerce hands: best to worst

**1. Three of a kind**

 beats

**2. Run:** a sequence in one suit

 beats

**3. Points:** the highest value using 2–3 cards of one suit

 beats

**BUT** if two hands are tied for Points value, three cards in one suit beats two in one suit:

 beats

**5.** Dealing passes to the **right**. If you run out of counters, you are out. Whoever wins all the counters wins.

# Gin rummy

| | |
|---|---|
| **Players** | 2 |
| **Difficulty** | Medium |
| **Deck** | 52 cards |
| **Extras** | Paper and pen to keep score |
| **Goal** | To meld most of your cards with the lowest remainder |
| **Ranks** | Aces are low |
| **Values** | Picture cards: 10; number cards: face value; Aces: 1 |

In this popular version of rummy (page 46), you finish when most of your cards are in matched sets or runs and the value of your remaining cards ('deadwood') is under ten.

**1.** Shuffle, and deal ten cards each. Deal one more face up to start the discard pile and place the rest face down to make a stock pile. The winner of each hand deals the next.

**2.** The non-dealer starts, **drawing a card** from the stock or top of the discard pile. If he doesn't want the card on the discard pile then on this first turn only the dealer can take it instead, **before** the non-dealer draws, discarding a card to replace it.

**3.** Each turn you try to gain a card that makes part of a **meld** (a set or run). **Sets** are 3–4 cards of the same rank. **Runs** are 3+ cards of the same suit in sequence. You then **discard a card.** You can't pick up a card from the discard pile and discard it in the same turn.

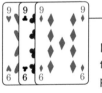

— Set

In this example, the 9♥ could be part of the set or the run, but not both at the same time.

— Run

**4. Going out** Take turns to draw and discard until one of you has a hand with enough melds and low enough deadwood. You then go out, if you want, by knocking, discarding a card face down, and laying out your melds. Going out with no deadwood at all is called 'going gin.'

**5. Scoring** If the **knocker went gin**, she wins the value of her **opponent's deadwood +25**. If not, he shows his melds then adds as many of his deadwood cards to her melds as he can. If the **knocker's deadwood ends up least**, she scores the **difference** between the two amounts.

But if his is the same or lower he has **undercut** her and scores the **difference +25**. First to **100 points wins**. If no-one knocks, the hand ends when two cards are left in the stock. Then it's a draw with no scores, and the next player deals.

**Example:** the end of a hand

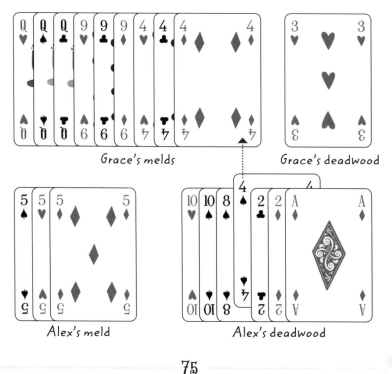

Grace's melds                    Grace's deadwood

Alex's meld                     Alex's deadwood

# Shed

| | |
|---|---|
| **Players** | 2–5 |
| **Difficulty** | Medium |
| **Deck** | 52 cards |
| **Goal** | To get rid of all your cards as soon as you can |
| **Ranks** | Aces are high |

This popular game has many names. The loser is often given a forfeit, such as being made to wear a silly hat.

**1.** Deal nine cards, one by one, to each player: a row of three face down, three face up on top of those, then three more face down, which they take as their hand. You play from your hand first, until it runs out, then from your face-up cards, and lastly from your face-down cards.

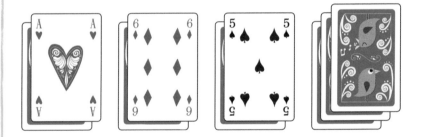

**2.** Put the rest face down in the middle to make a stock pile.

**3.** Players look at their hand and swap as many cards as they like with their face-up cards to create the highest set of face-up cards they can. (Wild cards are best: see page 77.)

**4.** The player left of the dealer goes first, starting the discard pile by placing any card face up on the table.

**5.** The next player must play a card of equal or higher rank, or, even better, a set of matching cards such as two 9s. She then draws from the stock until her hand is back up to three.

**6.** If the next player can't equal or beat the card on the pile, she has to pick the pile up.

## Special cards

2s are wild, so you can play them on any card, and any card can be played on them. Red 10s are also wild, but you can only play black 10s on anything under ten. After you play any 10, you remove the discard pile from the game, and get another turn.

**7.** If someone plays the final card(s) that completes a set of four matching cards on the discard pile, he can remove the discard pile and start a new one.

**8.** After the stock has run out and you have no cards in your hand, you move on to your face-up cards. If later you are forced to pick up cards, you must play from your hand before you return to your face-up cards.

**9.** When your face-up cards run out, you play blind with the face-down cards. If they don't match or beat the discard pile, you have to replace the face-down card and pick up the pile. (This can be infuriating if you're nearly out!)

**10.** When you get rid of all your cards, you have avoided becoming the loser and drop out of the game. The loser has to perform a silly forfeit, and becomes the next dealer.

# Bonkers

| | |
|---|---|
| **Players** | 3–5 |
| **Difficulty** | Medium |
| **Deck** | 4 players (32 cards): remove cards 2–6 from each suit; 3 or 5 players (30 cards): remove the black 7s, too |
| **Extras** | Paper and pen to keep score |
| **Goal** | To score the most points |
| **Ranks** | Aces are high |

Bonkers is really eight quick-fire games in one. In most rounds you try to lose certain tricks to avoid penalties, but in the last two you battle to win bonuses.

**1.** Cut the deck. Whoever has the lowest card deals first.

**2.** Shuffle, then deal ten cards each for three players, eight each for four, or six for five. The dealer moves clockwise with each round. In the first few rounds the dealer decides trumps, until everyone has chosen trumps once. There are no trumps in later rounds.

**3.** Each round has a different goal (see opposite), but the first five all work like this: the player to the dealer's left leads by playing any card. Everyone else must follow the leading suit if they can, but otherwise they can play any card. The highest card of the leading suit wins the trick, or the highest trump if any are played.

**4.** The winner of each trick leads the next. Keep your tricks as face-down piles. When all the cards have been played, work out the penalties and bonuses for each player (see page 79), then move on to the next round.

# Rounds 1-5

**Round 1: No Tricks** The dealer chooses trumps. The goal of the first round is not to win any tricks at all.
**Penalty:** -5 points per trick

**Round 2: No Hearts** The dealer chooses trumps. The goal is not to win any Hearts. You can't lead with Hearts unless you have no choice.
**Penalty:** -5 points per Heart card

**Round 3: No Boys** The dealer chooses trumps. The goal is not to win any Jacks or Kings. Leave any you win face up. The round ends as soon as they're all won.
**Penalty:** -5 points per Jack or King

**Round 4: No Girls** The dealer chooses trumps unless just three are playing, when this is not a trumps round. The goal is not to win any Queens. Leave any you win face up. The round ends as soon as they're all won.
**Penalty:** -10 points per Queen

**Round 5: No Last** This is not a trumps round unless five are playing. The goal is not to win the last trick.
**Penalty:** -20 points to the winner of the last trick

# Rounds 6-8

**Round 6: Hairy Ape** In this very silly round you don't look at your cards, but fan them back-to-front in your hands so that only the other players can see them. You then play each trick blind. The round ends as soon as the dreaded Hairy Ape (King♥) is won. **Penalty:** -20 points to the winner of the trick containing the King♥

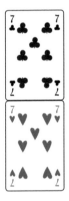

**Round 7: Dominoes** This round is like **Sevens** (page 21). Clear as much space as you can for the cards. The player left of the dealer starts by playing a card of any rank. Take turns to play the cards like dominoes, placing a card of the same suit and next rank to the left or right of a card, or one of the same rank above or below it. If you can play, you must. **Bonuses:** see Summary opposite

**Round 8: Bonkers** Shuffle the cards well after Dominoes, then total up the scores so far to see how everyone's doing. The last round is a crazy race to win as many bonus points as possible before the game ends. **Bonuses:** see Summary opposite

# Summary of rounds

**1. No Tricks**  Goal: don't win any tricks
(trumps)  Penalty: -5 per trick

**2. No Hearts**  Goal: don't win any Hearts
(trumps)  Penalty: -5 per ♥ card. You can't
lead with a ♥ unless you must.

**3. No Boys**  Goal: don't win any Jacks or Kings
(trumps)  Penalty: -5 per Jack or King

**4. No Girls**  Goal: don't win any Queens
(trumps*)  Penalty: -10 per Queen
*except when 3 play

**5. No Last****  Goal: don't win the last trick
Penalty: -20
**trumps only used when 5 play

**6. Hairy Ape**  Goal: don't win the King♥
Penalty: -20

**7. Dominoes**  Goal: go out first
Bonuses: 1st out: 20; 2nd out: 15;
3rd out: 5 (0 when 3 play)

**8. Bonkers**  Goal: win as many bonuses as you can
Bonuses: each trick: 5; each Jack or
King: 5 (except Jack♥: 10; King♥: 20)
each Queen: 10 (except Queen♥: 15);
Last trick: 20

# Durak

| | |
|---|---|
| **Players** | 2 |
| **Difficulty** | Medium |
| **Deck** | 36 cards (remove cards 2–5 from each suit) |
| **Goal** | To be first out of cards after the stock runs out |
| **Ranks** | Aces are high |

Durak is Russian for 'fool', because this game has no winner, just a loser. In each round, you either 'attack' or 'defend'.

**1.** Deal six cards each, three at a time. Put the rest face down to make a stock pile. Turn the top card face up to show trumps, then slide it face up halfway under the stock so you can still see it.

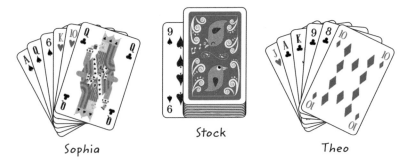

Sophia                    Stock                    Theo

**2.** The non-dealer is the first **attacker.** She can start with any card, but every card she then plays in that round has to **match a rank that has already been played.**

**3.** The **defender** must then beat the attack with a **higher card of the same suit, or a trump.** If he can't, then his defending fails and he has to add all the cards from that round to his hand. The attacker then attacks again in the next round.

**4.** If the attacker runs out of cards while the defender is unbeaten, or she doesn't have the cards she needs to continue, her attack fails. She puts all the cards played in the round aside, and will defend in the next round.

**5.** At the start of a new round make sure you have six cards – if not, draw more from the stock. The trump card counts as the last card of the stock and can be drawn. The game continues until just one player is holding cards – they are the Durak!

**Example of play: 2nd round** (Theo attacker, Sophia defender)

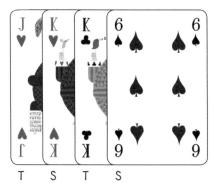

Theo's attack fails because he has no more Jacks or Kings, nor any 6s. He discards all the cards played in that round. Sophia becomes attacker.

**3rd round** (Sophia attacker, Theo defender)

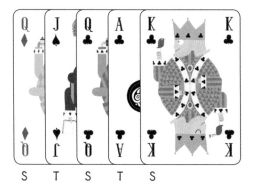

Sophia's attack succeeds because Theo has no high cards or trumps to beat her King ♣. Theo takes all the played cards into his hand.

# GOPS

| | |
|---|---|
| **Players** | 2 |
| **Difficulty** | Medium |
| **Deck** | 39 cards (sort into suits and remove the Hearts) |
| **Goal** | To win the most valuable Diamonds |
| **Values** | King: 13; Queen: 12; Jack: 11; number cards: face value; Ace: 1 |

'GOPS' stands for Game Of Pure Strategy. It is a game of skill and second-guessing where chance is not involved.

**1.** You each take all of one black suit and sort it in your hand. Shuffle the Diamonds and stack them face down.

**2.** Turn over the top Diamond. You both now 'bid' for it by choosing a card you think can win it and playing it face down. When you're both ready, reveal your cards. The highest wins the Diamond. If you tie, the Diamond is placed face up next to the Diamond pile and is won by the next outright winner.

**3.** The winner places the Diamond face up on their right, and their bid face up on their left. The cards in both piles should be overlapped so that both players can always see which ones have been played.

**4.** If the last bid is a draw, nobody wins it. The winner is the player whose Diamonds add up to the highest total.

# Yaniv

| | |
|---|---|
| **Players** | 2+ (best for 2–5) |
| **Difficulty** | Medium |
| **Deck** | 54 cards including Jokers (for 5+ players: 2 decks) |
| **Extras** | Paper and pen to keep score |
| **Goal** | To keep your score below 200 by having the lowest possible score at the end of each round |
| **Values** | Picture cards: 10; number cards: face value; Aces: 1 (Aces are low in runs); Jokers: 0 |

This gripping Israeli game has become very popular among backpackers, who have carried it all the way to the islands of Fiji and the mountains of Nepal.

**1.** Each player draws a card. The player with the lowest card leads (plays first). The player to her right deals.

**2.** Deal five cards each. The rest go in the middle to make a stock. Turn over the top card to start a discard pile.

**Example hands**
(mid-game)

Dan

Sarah

Sort your hands by
value, like this.

Jake

**3.** The lead player **discards** a card face up in front of her. This can be any single card, two or more cards of the same rank, or a run of three or more cards of the same suit, for example, Ace ♣, 2♣, 3♣. A Joker can stand in for any card.

**4.** She then **draws** a card from the stock or the discard pile. If the previous player discarded a run, she can draw its first or last card, but not from the middle.

**5.** She then puts her discarded card on the **discard pile.**

**6.** If at the start of your turn your hand is worth five points or less and you think it has the lowest value, you can call out "**Yaniv!**" This ends the round, and all show their cards.

### Example of final hands

Jake's hand is worth five, so he declares Yaniv.

Sarah

Dan

Jake

**7.** If the Yaniv caller has the lowest hand, he wins the round and scores 0. Everyone else scores the value of their hands. If another player has an **equal or lower hand**, then they call out "**Assaf!**" and whoever has the **lowest hand wins**. The Yaniv caller then scores his hand value +30.

## Scoring

Each player adds up his hand; one player keeps score.

| | |
|---|---|
| Correct Yaniv: | 0 points |
| Assaf: | 0 points |
| Incorrect Yaniv*: | 30 points + hand value |
| *with more than one equal Assaf: | 20 points per Assaf |
| All other players: | Hand value |

**8.** If the stock runs out, take all but the top card of the discard pile and shuffle it to make a new stock.

**9.** The winner leads the next round. If there are two, cut the deck and the one who draws the lowest card wins.

**10.** Keep playing rounds until one player's score goes over 200. For a short game, end the game there and say that whoever has the lowest score has won. For a longer game, say the high-scorer is knocked out and keep playing. The last player to keep her score under 200 is the winner.

**11.** If a player scores **exactly** 200, his score is halved to 100. If he scores exactly 100, his score is halved to 50.

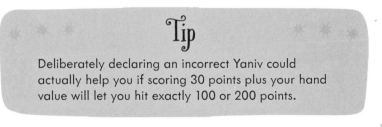

## Tip

Deliberately declaring an incorrect Yaniv could actually help you if scoring 30 points plus your hand value will let you hit exactly 100 or 200 points.

# Twenty-one

| | |
|---|---|
| **Players** | 3+ |
| **Difficulty** | Medium |
| **Deck** | 52 cards; 8+ players: two decks |
| **Extras** | 10 betting counters each (see page 110 for ideas) |
| **Goal** | To make a hand worth as near to 21 as you can, but no more, and to beat the banker |
| **Values** | Ace: 11 or 1; picture card: 10; number card: face value |

In this famous old betting game, also known as Blackjack, Vingt-et-un and Pontoon, suits don't matter – only values.

**1.** Pick someone randomly to be banker. She shuffles, and deals one card **face down** to each player, including herself.

**2.** You place bets in front of you depending on how confident you are of beating the banker (see hands in order of value below). The banker doesn't bet, or look at her card.

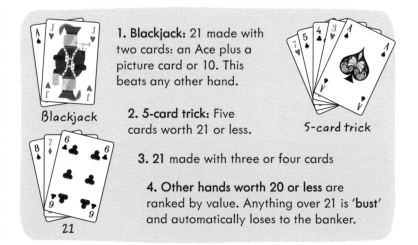

**1. Blackjack:** 21 made with two cards: an Ace plus a picture card or 10. This beats any other hand.

Blackjack

**2. 5-card trick:** Five cards worth 21 or less.

5-card trick

**3. 21** made with three or four cards

**4. Other hands worth 20 or less** are ranked by value. Anything over 21 is 'bust' and automatically loses to the banker.

21

**3.** The banker deals another card to each player **face up**, but hers **face down**. You all, including the banker, study your hand to decide how to play. Here are your options:

**Blackjack:** If you have a blackjack, you declare it, and turn the Ace face up on top of the face-down picture card.

**Stick** or **Stand:** If your hand is worth more than 15, you can choose to say "Stick" (or "Stand") and the next player takes his turn.

**Hit** or **Twist:** If you want to get closer to 21, you say "Hit" (or "Twist") and the dealer gives you a card **face up.** You can hit until you have five cards. If you go bust, you pay your bet to the banker.

**Buy** or **Double down:** If you haven't hit, you can instead say "Buy" (or "Double down") and increase your bet by anything from the original amount to twice that, and are dealt a card **face down.**

**Split:** If you have two matching cards you can say "Split", double your bet, and play them as two hands, one after the other, until you've stuck or gone bust with both.

**4.** If the banker has a blackjack, she shows it and the round ends. You all pay her double your bet. Otherwise you all play, starting from the banker's left.

**5.** On the banker's turn, she plays her hand face up for all to see, dealing to herself. She can **only hit or stick.** Then you all show your hands.

**7.** If the banker goes bust, she pays you the amount that you bet, or double for blackjacks and five-card tricks.

**8.** If the banker sticks on 21 or less, she pays bets to those who score more; double to blackjacks and five-card tricks. She wins the bets of all who score equal to or less than her.

**9.** If the banker scores a five-card trick, she pays double to blackjacks, but wins double bets from everyone else.

Example of play

Ellie's cards = 6.          Hit = 10          Hit = 18          Hit = 25: bust!

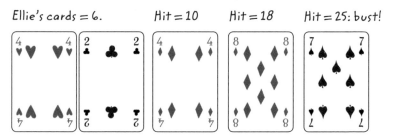

**10.** After a blackjack (unless it happened through a split) its player becomes the new banker, and shuffles the cards before the new deal. Otherwise, the banker gathers up the cards, places them under the deck, and deals again. If there is more than one blackjack, cut the deck and the one with the highest card becomes banker.

**11.** When one player runs out of counters, the player who then has the most counters wins. Or you can knock out players as they run out of counters until just one is left.

# Hearts

| | |
|---|---|
| Players | 4 |
| Difficulty | Medium |
| Deck | 52 cards |
| Extras | Paper and pen to keep score |
| Goal | To avoid winning Hearts or the Queen of Spades |
| Ranks | Aces are high |
| Points | Hearts: 1; Queen♠: 13; other cards: 0 |

Hearts score points in this game – but the lowest score wins.

1. Pick the first dealer. He shuffles, and deals all the cards.

2. At the start of the first round, you all pick **three cards** and pass them face down to the player on your **left**. In the next round, pass to the **right**; in the next, pass **across**; in the next, **don't pass**. Repeat this sequence as you play. If you have the Queen♠ or any high-ranking cards, pass them on.

3. Whoever has the 2♣ leads by playing it. You all follow suit, if you can. If you can't, you can play any card (except in the first trick you can't play the Queen♠ or a Heart). The highest card of the leading suit wins. The winner of each trick leads the next. Unless you have only Hearts, you can't lead with a Heart until Hearts have been played by someone who couldn't follow suit.

4. After each round, if you have won any tricks, add up any points from Hearts or the Queen♠. When someone gets to 100, the player with the fewest points wins. But if you win the Queen♠ and *all* the Hearts (26 points in all) you 'shoot the moon'. You score zero, and everyone else gets 26 points.

# Spades

| | |
|---|---|
| Players | 4 |
| Difficulty | Medium |
| Deck | 52 cards |
| Extras | Paper and pen to keep score |
| Goal | To win the number of tricks that your pair bids |
| Ranks | Aces are high; Spades are always trumps |

Spades is played with two pairs of partners who work together and sit opposite each other. At the start of each hand, you all make your own 'bid' saying how many tricks you think you will win. You and your partner then have to win at least as many tricks between you as your combined bid. If you under-bid or over-bid too often, though, you are penalized (see **Scoring**).

**1.** Choose a dealer. Shuffle the cards and deal them all to the players. There should be 13 each. The dealer moves clockwise at the start of each hand.

**2.** You all take turns to bid, from the dealer's left. A bid can be anything from 0 to 13 tricks. A **bid of 0** is called 'nil' and there is a **bonus** if you achieve it, but also a **penalty** if you do win any tricks. A nil bidder's partner must still win the number of tricks for which he has bid.

**3.** After the bids are declared, the player left of the dealer leads, playing anything but a Spade. You all follow suit if you can. If not, you can play any card.

**4.** The highest card of the leading suit wins, or the highest Spade if any are played. The winner of each trick leads the next. You can only lead with Spades after somebody has played one as a trump – unless you have only Spades.

**5.** The hand continues until all the cards have been played, then you count your tricks and work out your scores (see below). Play more hands until one team wins by reaching **500 points** or more. If both teams do at the same time, the highest score wins.

# Scoring

If a pair takes at least the **number of tricks it bid**, then it scores **ten times its bid**. Extra tricks, known as '**bags**', score **one point** each. If a pair does **not** reach its bid, it wins **no points** and **loses ten times its bid**.

If, over a number of rounds, a pair scores **ten bags**, they **lose 100 points**. This isn't hard to work out, as the 'ones' digits in a score show the bags piling up.

If a **nil bid succeeds**, the pair **scores 100 points**. If it **fails** they **lose 100 points**, and bags cannot be used as tricks by the partner. The partner still scores her points normally.

| Summary | Points |
|---|---|
| Tricks equal bid | 10 x bid |
| Tricks more than bid | 10 x bid +1 per bag |
| Tricks less than bid | –10 x bid |
| Ten bags | –100 |
| Succesful nil bid | +100 |
| Failed nil bid | –100 |

# Texas hold'em poker

| | |
|---|---|
| **Players** | 2–10 |
| **Difficulty** | Hard (easy to learn but hard to master) |
| **Deck** | 52 cards |
| **Extras** | Lots of counters (see page 110 for ideas) |
| **Goal** | To win the most counters |
| **Ranks** | Aces are high, but can count as low in sequences |

This is the most popular version of the world-famous betting game, poker. In Texas hold'em you place bets on how confident you are of making the best five-card hand. Don't worry if it seems complex at first – just give it a try.

Bets are usually placed using stackable counters called chips, which have different values, and are placed in a pile (**the pot**) in the middle. The winner takes the pot.

Gather as many counters as you can – anything that comes in different shades will do. Then agree on their values, e.g. **white: 1; red: 5; blue: 10.** You each might start with, say, ten white counters, four reds and two blues, giving everyone a total of **50.**

**1.** Choose a dealer. Shuffle well and deal everyone two cards face down. You're allowed to look at your cards, but **keep them secret.** Poker players often show who's dealer with a special white counter known as the Button. You can use anything you like.

# Poker hands: best to worst

**1. Royal flush:** Ace to Ten of the same suit in sequence

**2. Straight flush:** five cards of the same suit in sequence

**3. Four of a kind:** four cards of the same rank

**4. Full house:** three cards of the same rank plus a pair

**5. Flush:** five cards of the same suit

**6. Straight:** five cards of mixed suits in sequence

**7. Three of a kind:** three cards of the same rank

**8. Two pairs:** two pairs of matching cards

**9. Pair:** two cards of the same rank

**10. Highest card:** none of the above

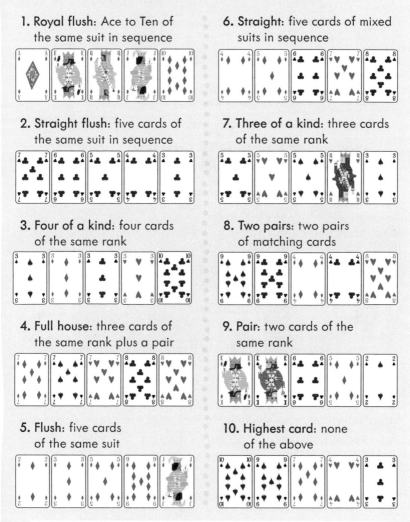

**Note:** In hands of the same type, the higher the cards used, the better. For example, a pair of Jacks beats a pair of 3s.

Aces can be high or low in sequences, but NOT both, so this would not be allowed: Q, K, A, 2, 3.

**2.** The two players left of the dealer always have to place 'blind' bets. This makes sure that somebody always bets. You all have to agree on a minimum bet – for example, two. The player left of the dealer places half the minimum bet, known as the **small blind.** The next player along places the **big blind,** the full minimum bet.

Start of example game showing dealer, small blind, big blind and poker player nicknames

**3.** First, you're going to learn how a **betting round** works, then see an example game that explains the rest. There are four betting rounds in a game. In the first, the only cards you can see are the two in your hand. In the second, you see three **community cards,** which are shared by everyone. The third and fourth rounds bring one more community card each.

Each betting round starts with the player on the dealer's left and goes around the table until everyone who still wants to bet has bet the same amount. Keep your bets in front of you until you've all decided what you will do, then put them into the pot. You have **four choices:**

- You can **call**. This means you put in enough counters to match the latest bet.

- You can **raise** the bet by paying as many more counters as you wish, after which everyone who wants to keep playing must call again.

- If no one has raised, you can **check**. This means you pay no more unless the bet is raised, and then you must either call again or fold.

- You can **fold**, which means that you are out of the game and lose everything you've bet so far. To fold, you put your cards face down into a group discard pile. You can't win a game by folding, but it's pointless to waste counters if your chances are very poor.

**4.** In the example game on page 96, the two blinds have started the **first betting round**, so The Kid is next. He studies his cards to decide if he wants to bet. High cards, pairs, cards next to each other in rank or cards of the same suit are all good. The Kid has the Queen and 9♣ (high, same suit and near in rank) so he decides to call, and pays two counters.

- Nico has the 7♠ and the 3♣. He knows they're not strong cards, but he **bluffs** (pretends they are). He calls, but also **raises** the bet by two, putting in four counters altogether.

- Texas Rose has a high card (King♥) and **calls**, paying four counters.

- The dealer, Corky, has a pair of 3s, and he calls too (four counters).

- Dolly, the small blind, decides that her cards aren't good enough, so she **folds.**

- Wild Bill, the big blind, has a high card and wants to bet. He calls by adding two counters to bring his bet up to four.

- The Kid still wants to bet so he calls, adding another two counters.

Now that everyone still betting has called, the dealer deals three community cards, known as **the flop,** face up in the middle:

Nico

Texas Rose

Corky

The pot

The flop

Discards

The Kid

Wild Bill

Dolly (folded)

**5.** The first betting player left of the dealer, Wild Bill, begins the **second betting round.** He doesn't want to raise, so he says "**check.**" The Kid checks too. Nico has a pair of 3s and raises the bet, adding two counters. Texas Rose sees she now has a pair of 4s, so she calls, adding two. Corky now has three of a kind (3s) so he calls, adding two. Wild Bill and The Kid fold. The dealer then deals the fourth community card: "**the turn.**"

The turn

**6.** The **third betting round** starts with Nico, who raises by two counters. Texas Rose sees that she now has two pairs, including a pair of Kings, so she calls, as does Corky, both putting in two more counters.

**7.** The dealer now deals the last community card, known as "**the river.**" The **fourth betting round** starts with Nico, who checks. Texas Rose sees that she now has a **full house** (three Kings and a pair of 4s) and raises the bet by four counters. Corky also sees that he has a full house (three 3s and a pair of Kings) so he calls, adding four. Nico folds.

*The river*

**8.** It's now the **showdown.** Texas Rose is the only player still in apart from the dealer, so she shows her cards first. Corky has lost because the larger part of Rose's full house is three Kings, beating his three 3s. He doesn't have to show his cards, but he does so that everyone can see that he had a full house, at least. If players show identical hands, for example a pair of Tens, the rank of the highest other cards, or '**kickers**', in their **five-card** hand decides who wins.

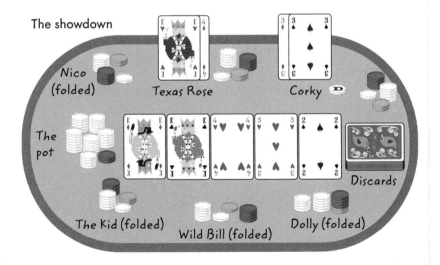

The showdown

Nico (folded)　　Texas Rose　　Corky

The pot

The Kid (folded)　　Wild Bill (folded)　　Dolly (folded)

Discards

Texas Rose's winning full house

Corky's full house

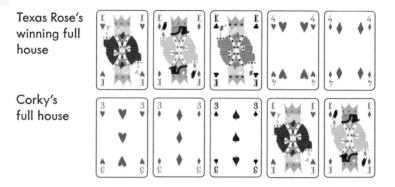

**9.** Dealing passes clockwise. Gather all the cards, shuffle, and play more games until somebody runs out of counters; whoever has the most counters then wins. Or you can continue playing until one player has won them all.

**10. Splitting the pot** If you want to call but don't have enough counters, you can "**go all in.**" This means you bet all the counters you have left, but if you win you only get back your bet from each player. Let's say that in a later game the pot already stands at 40. Corky raises by 25. Dolly and The Kid call. Nico only has 15 left, and goes all in. 15 chips from each bet go into the main pot, which Nico can win, and the extra 30 (ten from each of the others) go into a separate pot that Nico can't win. If Nico wins, he takes the main pot, and the second-best wins the 30. If he loses, the winner takes both pots.

## Poker tips

- It's tempting to bet if everyone else is, but it's wiser to fold soon if your hand is weak. "Live to fight another day."

- Don't bluff too much, but try to see if others are bluffing.

- The top six poker hands (page 95) come up less than 1% of the time. Half the time, your hand will just be 'highest card'. In Texas Hold'em, the winner often just has an Ace or King that is the highest kicker to two pairs or a pair.

# Canasta

| | |
|---|---|
| **Players** | 4 or 6 playing in teams of two |
| **Difficulty** | Hard |
| **Deck** | 108 cards (two 54-card decks including four Jokers) |
| **Extras** | Paper and pen to keep score |
| **Goal** | To score 5,000 points by building sets of cards |
| **Ranks** | Aces are high |
| **Values** | **2**: 20; **black 3**: 5; **red 3**: 100; **4–7**: 5; **8–King**: 10; **Ace**: 20; **Joker**: 50 |

Canasta is a rummy-like game from South America. Your main goal is to build matching sets called **melds**, especially seven-card melds, or **canastas**, which let you finish the game and score big bonus points. You also battle to pick up the discard pile, giving you more cards to score with. Canasta is usually played by four: two pairs working as partners. There are extra rules for six players at the end.

Each turn in canasta has three phases: you **draw a card**, then if you can, and you want to, you make **melds** (see page 102), and finally you **discard a card**. These cards are special:

**Jokers** are wild cards that can stand in for any card. Points: **50**

**2**s are wild cards too. Points: **20**

**Red 3**s are bonus cards. Play them as soon as you can. Points: **100**

**Black 3**s freeze the discard pile when they're on top of it. Points: **5** (see page 104)

**1.** All the other cards are known as **natural cards.** Natural cards up to 7 are worth **5 points.** From 8 up to King are worth **10 points.** Aces are worth **20 points.**

**2.** Each team works together to make melds, which stay on the table, and to build them into canastas. A team's melds are laid in front of one partner.

**3.** A **meld** must contain at least **three cards,** all of the same rank, laid in a column. At least two must be natural, and no more than three can be wild, so you can't make a whole meld out of wild cards.

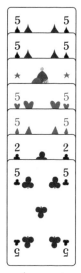

*A mixed canasta*

**4.** A canasta is a meld of **seven cards** (or more) so at least four must be natural cards. **Completed canastas** are stacked into piles with a red card face up on top for a **pure canasta** (all natural cards) worth **500 points,** or a black card for a **mixed canasta** (containing wild cards) worth **300 points.** You can still add to completed canastas, but change the top card to black if a pure canasta becomes mixed.

## Tip

Games like canasta involve handling lots of cards. To make this easier, you can split your hand into two hands, picking them up one at a time. If you have a choice of decks to play with, go for 'Bridge' size cards, which are smaller than 'Poker' size.

**5. Starting the game** Split the deck between the players so everyone can help to shuffle. Then deal 11 cards each. Stack the rest face down as the stock, and turn up the top card to start a discard pile. If the top card is a wild card (Joker or 2) place it in the discard pile so that it sticks out sideways (this shows the pile is 'frozen' – see page 104). Then turn up another card and place it on top the usual way around. If the top card is a red 3, bury it in the stock and draw another.

Example hands

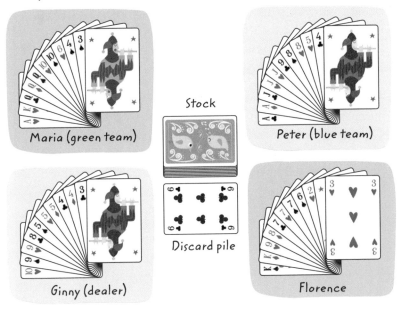

Maria (green team)

Stock

Peter (blue team)

Ginny (dealer)

Discard pile

Florence

**6. Draw** The player left of the dealer draws from the stock.

**7. Meld** She now makes as many melds as she likes. In later turns she will also be able to add cards to melds that she or her partner have already played. You can meld the same rank as another team but a team cannot have more than one meld of the same rank. The first meld or melds each team plays must have a combined card value of at least **50**.

**8. Discard** She then discards one card to the discard pile. Wild cards must be placed in the discard pile so they stick out sideways. The next player then begins his turn.

# Picking up the discard pile

Once your team has played its first meld, you can then draw from the discard pile as well as from the stock. You can only do this if you immediately play its top card in a meld, and you then get to pick up the whole discard pile. You can't use other cards in the discard pile to make this particular meld, but you can then go on to meld as much as you like with your enlarged hand.

Picking up the discard pile is your first goal in the game, as it gives you the pick of the cards, but it's a risk later on if you think your opponents are about to end the game, because any cards left in your hand at the end will cost you penalty points.

If the discard pile contains a **wild card,** it is **frozen.** This means you can't pick it up unless you have at least **two natural cards in your hand** that can make a new meld with the top card. You can't just add the top card to an existing meld. As soon as you pick up the pile, it is unfrozen.

If the discard pile has a **black 3 on top it is frozen.** You can't meld with 3s, so you can't pick it up at all until it's covered by another card. Use black 3s to prevent the next player from taking the discard pile. It's best to hold on to them until later in the game when freezing the discard pile can really help you.

## Example of play
(mid-game)

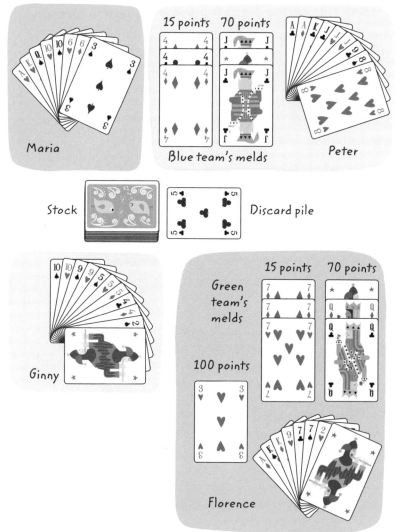

Maria

**15 points** **70 points**

Blue team's melds

Peter

Stock

Discard pile

Ginny

Green team's melds

**15 points** **70 points**

**100 points**

Florence

**9. Going out** You keep playing, building melds and canastas until someone 'goes out' by discarding their last card, thus scoring **100 points.** If you go out **without any canastas** you **lose** 100 points.

**10. Permission** You don't have to, but you can ask your partner's permission before you go out so she can make sure that she doesn't have too many high-value cards in her hand, costing your team penalty points. You can ask before or after you draw, but if you do, then you must go on to do what your parter says.

**11.** On going out, and only then, you can **meld with black 3s** (which are not natural cards) but no wild cards can be included.

**12.** You get **100 bonus points** if you go out by playing a **concealed canasta.** This is when you play your entire hand in one turn, including a canasta, either discarding one card as usual, or melding them all. It is only allowed if you have yet to make, or add to, any melds. It's hard to do, because you don't get any help from your partner.

**13. End of the game** A hand also ends if the stock has run out when somebody wants to draw from it, or if the last card of the stock is a red 3: it is laid down and the hand is over. Keep playing, the dealer moving clockwise, until one team wins by reaching **5,000 points.**

**14. Opening melds** The first meld each team plays in any game has a minimum value. As your team's score reaches certain levels, so does the minimum:

| Score | Minimum opening meld |
|---|---|
| Negative | 0 |
| 0–1,495 | 50 |
| 1,500–2,995 | 90 |
| 3,000+ | 120 |

# Canasta scoring

At the end of each round, use this table to find your team's score, which can be negative (in minus points).

| | |
|---|---|
| Total value of your melded cards | See **Values** on page 101 |
| Natural canasta | 500 points each |
| Mixed canasta | 300 points each |
| Going out | 100 points |
| Going out with concealed canasta | An extra 100 points |
| Red 3 with a canasta | 100 points each |
| All four red 3s with a canasta | An extra 400 points |

| | |
|---|---|
| Total value of cards left in your hands | **Subtract** this value |
| Going out with no canastas | -100 points |
| Red 3 with no canastas | -100 points each |
| All four red 3s with no canastas | An extra -400 points |
| Red 3 left in your hand | -500 points |

**15. Six-player Canasta** This version uses three decks shuffled together, with six Jokers. You can either play as three teams of two, seated 123123, or as two teams of three, seated 121212. Deal 13 cards each, and the first team to 10,000 points wins. At the end of a hand, five red 3s score a bonus of 1,000; all six score 1,200. When your score reaches 7,000, your minimum opening meld (see Point 14) is 150.

## Tips

Don't meld too much, or you may be forced to discard cards you want to keep. If you keep two matching natural cards in hand, you may be able to pick up the discard pile when it's frozen.

# Words used in card games

### Ace
This card may **rank** as the lowest card ('Aces are low') or rank above a King ('Aces are high').

### Bluffing
Pretending to have better or worse cards than you really do

### Bury
To slide a card randomly into the middle of the **stock**

### Cutting the deck
**1.** Lifting up a number of cards from a **face**-down **deck** to reveal the face of one card, for example, to choose dealer.
**2.** Swapping two portions of the deck as an extra shuffle.

### Deal
To hand out the required number of cards to the players. Unless the rules say otherwise, starting from the player to your left, hand them out face down, one by one, clockwise until every player has the right number. Take turns to deal, also clockwise. You can choose the dealer by dealing one card each and seeing whose is highest.

### Deck
A full set of English playing cards has 52 cards with 13 cards in each **suit**. Sometimes two **Jokers** are included, making 54 cards. Decks from some countries contain different numbers of cards. Games in this book that use those decks show you how to make an English deck 'shorter' or 'longer' as needed.

### Discard
To remove a card from your **hand**. It may be placed **face** up in a discard pile next to you, or in a shared discard pile.

## Face

The front side of a card, showing its rank. If cards are 'face down' you can only see their backs. **Face value** means that the **value** of a number card is the same as its **rank**.

## Follow suit

To play a card of the same suit as another card.

## Foundation

In patience or solitaire games, foundations are piles that you build up by adding cards in rank order.

## Go out

Play your last card

## Hand

**1.** The group of cards a player holds fanned out in his hand, so he only can see them.
**2.** A round of a game in which all the cards in the players' hands are played.

*Alternating red and black suits in your hand makes it easier to see what you have.*

## Jokers and wild cards

Two extra cards that look different from the number or picture cards. In most games they are left out, but in some games they are special trumps, or else '**wild cards**' that can stand in for any card a player needs.

## Kings, Queens and Jacks

The picture (or 'court') cards. They **rank** above the number cards, and usually have a higher **value**.

## Leading

The leading player is the one who plays first. The leading card is the card she plays, and the leading suit is its **suit**.

## Pot

In betting games, a pile of counters contributed to by each player that makes up the winner's prize.

### Things you can use as counters

buttons • flat beads • toothpicks • dried beans or pasta
gummy bears • board game pieces, tiles or toy money
paperclips • jigsaw puzzle pieces • tiddlywinks discs
coins • toy plastic bricks • bottletops • jelly beans

**Rank** is the order of the cards. A Jack ranks above a 10, a Queen above a Jack, and a King above a Queen. (see also **Ace**)

## Run

A sequence of three or more cards in rank order: 8♣, 9♦, 10♣, Jack♠. In some games, such as rummy, runs must contain cards of the same suit.

## Set

A group of three or four cards of the same **rank**: 3♥, 3♠, 3♦.

## Shuffle

To mix up a **deck** of cards into a random order before they are **dealt**. Here are some easy ways to shuffle:

**Scramble**

Just spread out the cards face down on the table, move them around, then pick them all up again.

**Pile shuffle**

For an extra-thorough shuffle, after shuffling deal the cards one by one into three piles, then stack them again.

## Overhand shuffle

**1.** Hold the deck in one hand, the long edge upwards, loosely held in place with your thumb.

**2.** With the thumb and middle finger of your other hand, lift a portion of cards from the deck.

**3.** Drop them lightly so that the cards from the two piles mix. Repeat several times.

## Stock
A face-down pile of cards from which new cards are drawn.

## Suits and pips
There are four suits in a **deck** of cards. Each has symbols called **pips** with distinctive designs.

♥ Hearts     ♣ Clubs

♦ Diamonds     ♠ Spades

## Trick
In some games, such as whist, you aim to win the cards all the players have played in one turn. These cards together are called a trick, and to win them is to 'take the trick.' Players usually keep their tricks in little piles.

## Trump suit
A suit that beats all other suits in certain games. For example, if Hearts are trumps, the lowest Heart beats the highest card of any other suit.

**Value** is the number a card is worth, often for scoring points.

## Work pile
In patience or solitaire games, work piles are piles of cards you can play to and from as you try to achieve your goal.

# Index of games

Advanced snap **7**

Animal snap **16**

Baroness patience
 see *Thirteens*

Blackjack
 see *Twenty-one*

Black Maria
 see *Hearts*

Blink **5**

Bonkers **78**

Boodle see *Stops*

Botheration see
 *Oh well!*

Bristol solitaire **41**

Canasta **101**

Catch the Ten **43**

Chase the Ace **19**

Cheat **18**

Chinese Ten **44**

Commerce **72**

Concentration
 see *Pairs*

Crazy Eights **54**

Cuckoo see *Chase
 the Ace*

Cucumber **49**

Domino see *Sevens*

Donkey see *Pig*

Durak **82**

Egyptian rat slap **58**

Fan Tan see *Sevens*

Five piles see *Thirteens*

Garbage **66**

Gin rummy **74**

Go boom **12**

Go fish **10**

Golf **38**

GOPS **84**

Hearts **91**

I doubt it see *Cheat*

James Bond **22**

Jig see *Snip
 Snap Snorum*

Jubilee **50**

Kings' corners **56**

Knockout whist **62**

Linger longer **26**

Martha patience **42**

Michigan see *Stops*

Muggins **32**

Nerts see
 *Racing demon*

Newmarket see *Stops*

Oh well! **64**

Old maid **8**

Pairs **9**

Pig **14**

Pip-Pip! **70**

Poker see *Texas
 hold'em poker*

Pontoon
 see *Twenty-one*

Pounce see
 *Racing demon*

President **30**

Racing demon **60**

Ranter go round *see
 Chase the Ace*

Rolling stone **24**

Rummy **46, 48, 74**

Scotch whist see
 *Catch the Ten*

Scum see *President*

Sevens **21**

Shed **76**

Slapjack **20**

Snap **6, 7, 16**

Snip Snap Snorum **34**

Spades **92**

Spoons **15**

Stealing bundles **28**

Stops **68**

Switch see
 *Crazy eights*

Ten-Ten-Five-One **36**

Texas hold'em poker
 **94**

Thirteens **40**

Thirty-one **52**

Trumps see
 *Knockout whist*

Twenty-one **88**

Vingt-et-un
 see *Twenty-one*

Whist **62**

Yaniv **85**

Cover designed by Karen Tomlins

With thanks to Joyce Brown and Sam Smith

First published in 2015 by Usborne Publishing Ltd, 83–85 Saffron Hill, London EC1N 8RT, England. Copyright © 2015 Usborne Publishing Ltd. The name Usborne and the devices ♀♡ are Trade Marks of Usborne Publishing Ltd. All rights reserved.